Golf Step-by-Step

Golf Step-by-Step

The Indispensable Guide On How To Play The Game

Mel Sole

SALAMANDER

Produced in 2002 by
PRC Publishing Ltd,
64 Brewery Road, London N7 9NT
A member of **Chrysalis** Books plc

Published by Salamander Books Limited
64 Brewery Road, London, N7 9NT
A member of **Chrysalis** Books plc

All correspondance concerning the content of this book should
be addressed to Salamander Books Ltd.

ISBN 1 84065 431 7

Printed and bound in China

CONTENTS

PREFACE 6

INTRODUCTION 8

EQUIPMENT 12

CLOTHES AND ACCESSORIES 24

TEACHING AIDS 32

THE VALUE OF TAKING LESSONS 40

STRETCHING, EXERCISING, AND WARMING UP 44

STARTING OUT 56

THE SWING 74

FAIRWAY WOODS 92

PITCHING 102

CHIPPING 112

PUTTING 122

HAZARDS AND TROUBLE SHOTS 132

FAULTS AND PROBLEM-SOLVING 168

COURSE MANAGEMENT 216

MENTAL ATTITUDE 220

JUNIORS', SENIORS', AND WOMEN'S GOLF 228

NUTRITION 238

RULES AND ETIQUETTE 242

TEN FAVORITE COURSES 249

INDEX 255

PREFACE

After teaching golf to people all ages and skill levels for some 30 years it seems timely that I share what I've learned in the form of a book. My goal is to introduce you to a wonderful and fascinating game and to help instruct you on the skills needed for you to enjoy playing it. My ultimate aim is that you'll learn to love golf and make it a lifetime pursuit.

Instructions and photographs will guide you through the fundamentals, from techniques for the full swing and the magic of the short game to the mental aspects of golf. Learn the rules, understand etiquette, exercises to do beforehand, the best types of food to eat, the history of golf, and more.

Golf is very much a game of patience. It takes time and practice to create good habits within your golf swing. As with any other skill in life—whether athletic, musical, mental, or suchlike—practice instills confidence and once confidence is gained it leads to hours of enjoyment.

Enjoy your journey and tee it up often!

Mel Sole, Director of Instruction,
The Phil Ritson-Mel Sole Golf School ,
Pawleys Island, South Carolina.

INTRODUCTION
A Brief History of the Game

There has been much discussion on where and when golf started. The Scots are undoubtedly the custodians of the game. However, some experts agree that the game most likely developed in Holland from a game called "kolven," which was played with a curved stick much like a hockey stick but using a round ball —a cross between ice hockey and field hockey. There are records of matches played as far back as 1297.

Golf in Scotland started at least before 1450, where there were records of King James II banning the playing of "gouf" and enforcing archery practice, which was regarded as a more useful skill in times of war. There are also records of King James IV of Scotland playing golf in 1502 when he had a set of clubs made for him by a bow maker from Perth. And in 1567 Mary Queen of Scots was chastised for playing soon after the death of her husband.

The popular theory behind the origins of golf begins when Dutch sailors came over to Scotland bringing their trading goods with them. To get to the pub, which was in town about a mile and a half inland, the sailors devised a game using "kolven" sticks to hit a ball to the pub, the loser having to buy the drinks for that night. On returning to the ship they were too drunk to keep a continuous score, so they divided the distance back to their ship into equal sections, creating the "inward" and "outward" holes to their ship.

The same holes were used for both directions, but as the popularity of the game increased, this became a problem, as it took much longer to play. Therefore, additional holes were cut in the green for the inward and outward players and to this day there are still seven greens at St. Andrews that contain two holes. These huge double greens can cause players to have putts of up to 90 yards if the ball lands on the wrong side of the green.

During the early 15th century, the local townspeople continued the tradition, and over time the Old Course at St. Andrews developed. In 1592, there was a proclamation against golf being played on a Sunday, to make sure people attended church. To this day, St. Andrews is closed on Sunday and the course is used as a public park for all the townspeople to enjoy.

ABOVE: Golfers enjoy an afternoon at Blackheath Golf Club in this humorous sketch made in 1863.

PREVIOUS PAGE: An elegant gentleman plays golf accompanied by his caddy in a painting by Lemuel Francis Abbott from about 1790.

In 1754, The Society of St. Andrews' Golfers was established and the course, at that time, had 22 holes. In 1764, the committee determined that four of the holes were "too short" and by combining a few holes, they introduced the current 18-hole format.

In the 18th century, 12 other clubs were established, the earliest of which was the Gentleman Golfers of Leith, later to become the honorable Company of Edinburgh Golfers. They established the original 13 Rules of Golf in 1744. In 1834, King William IV became the patron of The Society of St. Andrews' Golfers and changed the title to the Royal and Ancient Golf Club of St. Andrews.

The first British Open was played in 1860 at Prestwick, where it was played for the next 13 years. The venues later included St. Andrews and Musselburgh, and then much later, Muirfield and Hoylake. The original first tee still stands at Prestwick today, and the 17th hole is the only unchanged hole from the original design, although some of the original greens and tees remain. Golf did not really start in England until the 17th century when King James VI of Scotland ascended the throne as King James I and started to play golf at Blackheath Common on the outskirts of London.

Ladies entrance into golf began in 1868 with the North Devon Ladies Club, which had its own nine-hole course. Only putting was allowed as it was regarded as unladylike to swing the club above shoulder height; the clothing of the day seemed to prohibit more than that anyway. The Ladies Golf Union was founded in 1893.

Golf was soon spreading to the far corners of the globe, such as the Royal Calcutta in India, which became the oldest club outside of the United Kingdom. Royal Montreal was the first club established on the North American continent in 1873 and St Andrews Club in Yonkers, New York, is regarded as the first club established in the United States.

The Walker Cup in 1922 introduced international competition between British and American male amateurs. A few years later, the Ryder Cup (1927) fostered competition between British (later European) and American male professionals. The Curtis Cup (1932) established a competition between British and American female amateurs, and finally the Solheim Cup included professional female players from Europe and America. In 1971, golf went beyond the bounds of an international sport and truly became "out of this world," when Alan Shepard hit the first golf shot on the moon with a six iron.

Golf courses are rapidly being built throughout the world, which indicates the popularity of the game. Men, women, and children of all ages are taking up golf. Accessibility has never been easier, and instructional programs are tailored to suit the requirements of juniors, women, beginners, and advanced players. Golf professionals and top amateurs alike are striving harder to excel. They work out daily to improve their athletic performance, consult sports psychologists to improve their mental toughness, and also see dieticians for better health and endurance.

Golf will continue to grow. As technology improves, the Royal and Ancient Club of St. Andrews and the United States Golf Association continually monitor both the rules and development, to ensure that the honesty and integrity of the game will be upheld for generations to come.

BELOW: British Golfers play at St Andrews in Scotland in the late 19th century.

EQUIPMENT

Golf equipment has dramatically developed and advanced like no other sport. Soccer, football, ice hockey, and basketball have all been played with reasonably similar equipment since those games began. However, golf has gone from feathery balls and hazel shafted irons to the multimaterial wonders that we see today.

Golf balls were originally made with an outer layer of leather and the inside consisted of the amount of feathers it took to fill a top hat. These feathers were boiled and then stuffed into a leather pouch with a stick. The pouch was sewn up and hammered into a round ball. A single ball would take a day to make and were beyond the means of ordinary people, making it a rich man's game. Weather was a factor, because if the ball got wet it would be heavier and would not fly as far, and was also more likely to split open. Putting also became a challenge as the balls would not hold their round shape for very long.

The clubheads of the day were made of blackthorn or beach and the shafts were made of hazel. They were longer and shallower than today's clubs. These were used along with the feathery ball for some 400 years until 1848 when the first major breakthrough came with the invention of the gutta ball. This ball was far cheaper to manufacture and many could be made in a day bringing the price down considerably. Now more people could enjoy a pleasure that was previously out of their price range. Golfers found that as a ball got older it flew better, and so the aerodynamic properties of the ball were discovered. Various markings and patterns on the ball started to appear at this time.

This new ball had an effect on the clubs, as the harder ball damaged the wooden faces of the clubs, making the fairly rigid wooden shafts shatter. Leather inserts were introduced and hickory was used to allow more give in the shafts. Iron heads were developed for hitting trouble shots out of gorse and tree roots. So began the introduction of the mid iron, cleek, niblick and mashie, which gave the golfer several more clubs.

In the late 1890s, a gentleman by the name of Haskell developed a rubber-wound ball that would fly 20 to 30 yards further. (The golfer's quest for distance still has not changed in over a hundred years.) In 1902, Alec Heard won the Open Championship at Hoylake using this new ball, which signaled the end of the gutta percha era. Again a much harder wood was needed to handle the new ball so persimmon was

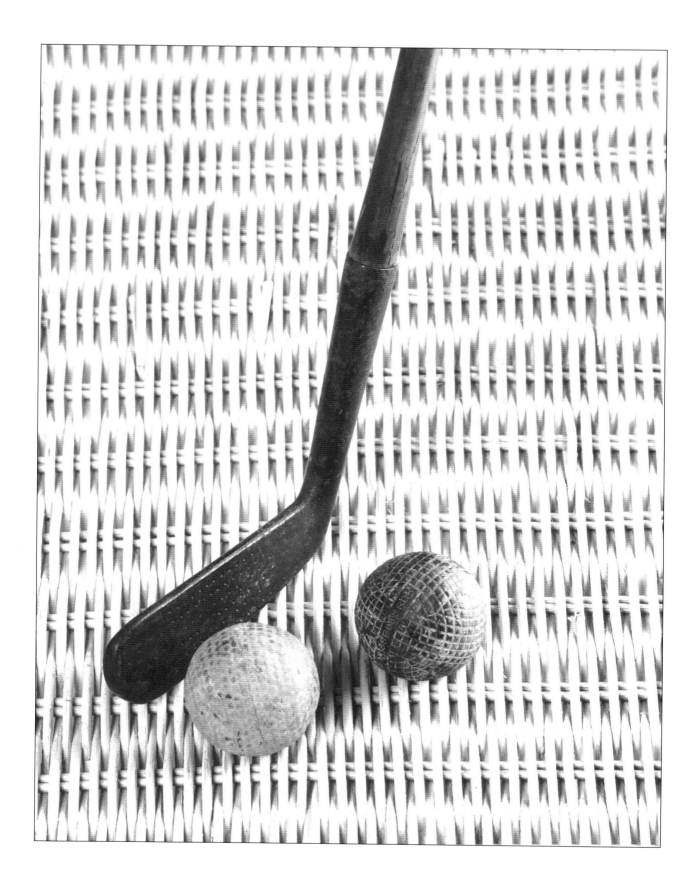

RIGHT: The forged blade irons (top) are popular with lower handicap golfers, while the investment cast perimeter weighted irons (bottom) are more popular with higher handicap golfers as they are easier to hit.

BELOW RIGHT: Clubs have progressed from the long-nosed baffie of the 1800s (right) to the persimmon clubs of the early to mid 1990s (center) to the modern titanium driver (left) with a multi-material shaft.

introduced for the wooden clubs. Brass and metal sole plates were added to protect these clubs. As demand for this wood increased a shortage in supply resulted so laminated woods and eventually steel-headed woods were created.

After World War I, with hickory being in short supply, steel shafts were introduced, and painted to look like hickory. This proved to be a tremendous advancement in golf club equipment and the steel shaft was used in competition for the first time in the United States in 1926 and in Britain in 1930.

The number of clubs available to the player was getting out of hand, so in 1930 a rule was introduced by both the Royal and Ancient Golf Club (R&A) and the U.S. Golf Association to limit the number of clubs a golfer could carry in their bag. They settled on 14, a rule which stands to this day.

Improvements in golf ball development also forced the ruling bodies to set limits on the initial velocity of the ball to 260ft per second. They believed that limiting the speed with which the ball leaves the clubface would limit the distance it would travel. This was not the case especially after the advent of new dimple patterns that increased the amount of "airtime," resulting in a greater distance.

There will always be rivalry between the manufacturers who need advancements to help sell their equipment and the ruling bodies, who are attempting to keep the game in some sort of check. However, without ruling bodies, great golf courses would become extinct and new courses would be built that are longer and tougher, ultimately making the game unenjoyable for the average golfer who has been the backbone of this sport for centuries.

Choosing a set of 14 golf clubs may seem difficult for the beginner, so a selection of modern clubs are outlined below.

WOODS 1 THROUGH 9

Woods evolved and progressed from the long-nosed clubs of the 1800s to the beautiful persimmon woods used until the mid 1980s when steel-headed woods were introduced. Titanium drivers and fairway woods are recent developments.

IRONS 1 THROUGH 9

A pitching wedge is usually about 50 degrees, a sand wedge is usually about 55 degrees, and a lob wedge about 60 degrees. Irons have progressed from forged ones, which were stamped out from a single piece of steel, to investment cast ones, where a liquid metal is poured into a mold. This new process allows toe-heel and perimeter weighting that was not possible previously.

Forged clubs are used by touring professionals and better players, who feel the contact off a clubface is more consistent and therefore gives them better control. These

RIGHT: "Utility clubs" that help the average golfer get the ball into the air more easily are becoming a popular choice.

clubs, however, leave a very small margin of error and are not ideal for the high hand-icap player. With investment cast clubs, the weight is distributed more towards the outer part of the clubface allowing a larger sweet spot and making it a more forgiving club.

There are also hybrid clubs. Some clubs look like irons but perform like woods and other clubs look like woods but perform like irons. All this can be very confusing to the beginner so it is always best to seek professional advice before purchasing a new set of clubs.

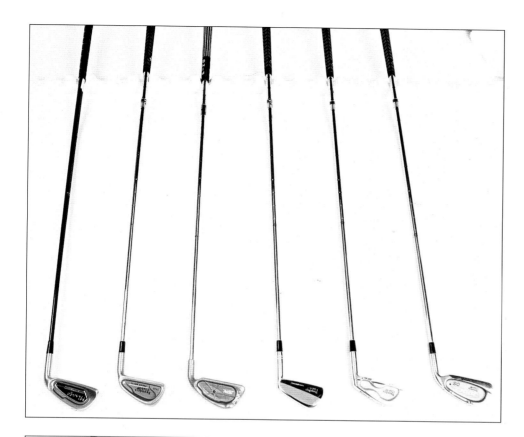

LEFT: Manufacturers design irons to achieve goals of "higher flight" or "more distance" or even "better feel." Take your pick.

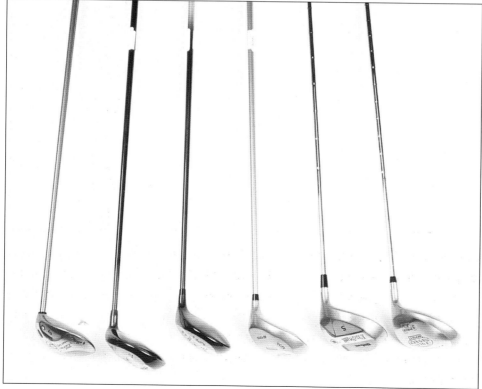

LEFT: Metal woods are made with similar design goals in mind.

RIGHT: Sand wedges are designed to have various "bounce" features.

RIGHT: An example of some of the many pitching, sand, and lob wedges.

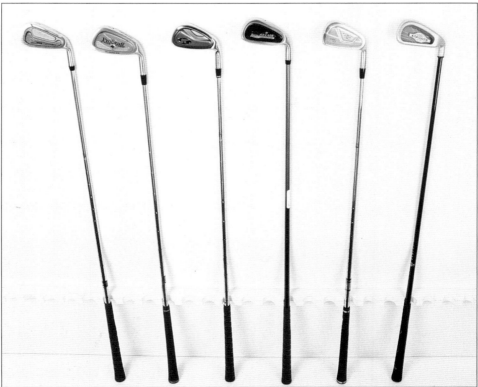

SHAFTS

Shafts have progressed from hickory to steel to fiberglass and finally to graphite. Once again the better players prefer steel, but the lightness of graphite allows more weight to be put into the head, which produces more distance for the high handicapper. The manufacturing process of graphite shafts has become an art unto itself producing shafts of varying flexes and kick points. Seek professional help when looking for a shaft that is perfect for your game.

BELOW: A beginner's set of three woods, four irons, and a putter is an inexpensive way to get started.

BOTTOM: Shafts come in all types of flexes and kick points to suit all levels.

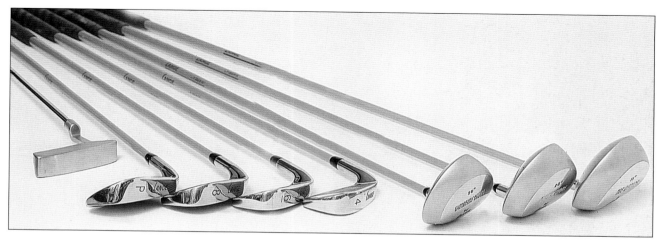

GRIPS

Grips can be made of leather, rubber, or other synthetic materials, or any combination of these. Often golfers pay little attention to the grip, but a good connection with the club is important for developing a strong technique. If you are to build a good, solid, swing then your grip must feel comfortable. Try out several types of grips before deciding what feels right for you.

ABOVE: Rubber grips are suitable in all types of weather.

RIGHT: Leather grips tend to give a "softer" feel.

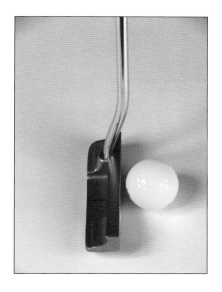  

ABOVE LEFT: A toe/heel balanced putter.

ABOVE CENTER: A blade putter has a shaft that enters at the neck.

ABOVE RIGHT: A mallet putter has a larger head.

RIGHT: The long putter has become popular with senior golfers.

PUTTERS

Putters come in all shapes and sizes but the three pictured (top) are the most common. The toe-heel balanced putter prevents the club from twisting through impact, the blade putter is popular with low handicap players, and the mallet, with its long line perpendicular to the face, helps with alignment.

Putters also come in different lengths, but the standard is 36in. The long putter has become popular with senior players and those who have the yips (a nervous twitch) and struggle with those short three footers.

GOLF BALLS

Golf balls have also become extremely high-tech and multilayer and multi-material balls can be found for sale in every golf shop. Each manufacturer claims that their ball goes 20 yards further. The truth of the matter is that all top balls go about the same distance, so again, ask a professional for advice on which ball will best suit your game and your wallet. Another overlooked part of the golf equipment evolution is the lawnmower. These engineering marvels can now cut fairways and greens to exact specifications, and the putting surfaces of today are as smooth as billiard tables. Therefore putting is much easier and because of the precise setting of the mowers, the greens are consistent from the first hole to the 18th.

Two other pieces of equipment worth noting are shoes and gloves (see also pages 26–27). It is not certain when golfers started to wear gloves for a better grip, but this has definitely helped prevent clubs from slipping out of many a pair of hands on hot and humid summer days. Spikes in shoes were introduced in the 1930s to improve traction and balance. There were no significant changes until the early 1990s when "soft" or plastic spikes were introduced. These limited the amount of wear and tear that the metal spikes were causing on the greens, leaving the surface smoother and allowing for easier putting shots.

RIGHT: A multi-layered ball gives a combination of spin and feel.

CHOOSING EQUIPMENT

Although the mechanics of the golf swing is the first and foremost factor in hitting a good golf shot, using the right equipment will certainly maximize your talents.

There are several factors to consider when choosing equipment. It is important first of all to try several demo clubs, each having different specifications, to help you decide on the right set of clubs. However, the following elements need to be taken into consideration:

1. **LENGTH:** The most important club specification is appropriate length. The right club length for your height and stature allows you to assume the correct address position, without which a proper golf swing can't be executed. The length of the club is primarily determined by the distance from the fingertips to the ground. However, since strength and athletic ability are also important factors in determining club length, it is to your benefit to seek the advice of a professional. If you want a little more distance off the tee, add an inch to your driver. This will allow a slightly bigger arc and help to generate a little more clubhead speed.

2. **SHAFT FLEX:** Many players have shafts that are too stiff for them. There are many choices of both steel and graphite shafts, so try them out. Hit shots with different shafts and flexes and note distance, trajectory, and direction.

3. **GRIP THICKNESS:** Have your instructor check your grip to make sure your hands fit snugly and comfortably on the club.

4. **SWING WEIGHT:** Swing weight is affected by length, which will affect shaft flex. The proper swing weight will be determined after deciding the first two factors.

5. **LIE ANGLE:** The most overlooked and probably the most important aspect of your irons is the lie angle. Most golfers have clubs that are too flat, causing the toe of the club to hit the ground first, opening the clubface and resulting in a slice or push. Note the depths of your divots. Is the toe of the divot deeper than the heel? This will indicate that the club lie angle is too flat. The opposite will be true of heel-deep divots, although this is not so common.

You don't necessarily have to buy new clubs, you can have your clubs altered by a professional club fitter. Finally, don't fall for any advertising hype that tells you what to buy for a better game. Let common sense prevail and seek good advice.

CLOTHES AND ACCESSORIES

Since golf's earliest days apparel has been of the utmost importance to golfers—as much to look good as to allow easy and comfortable play. Early Scots considered tail coats to be de rigueur on the course, while in the early part of the 20th century golfers typically dressed in plus-twos or plus-fours with long and colorful argyle socks. Their outfit was usually completed with a jaunty cap. The 1960s and 1970s were a time of great flamboyance in the golfing world, and startling plaids were all the rage. For the most part today's golfers are more subdued in their tastes, while technology provides 21st century clothing that is as engineered to provide comfort as it is stylish.

Shirts and sweaters manufactured from space-age materials are light and allow the skin to breathe and keep perspiration at bay. At the same time they are wind and rain resistant and will keep the golfer warm in less balmy climates. Such clothing is also specially cut to ensure that there is no impediment to the swing.

ABOVE, RIGHT AND OPPOSITE: Pro shops carry all the clothing and accessories a golfer needs.

SHOES AND SPIKES

Traditionally golf shoes were fitted with steel cleats on the bottom to provide golfers with the traction that they often need. These days course superintendents require all golfers to wear shoes without spikes in order to protect the fragile greens. In response to this, shoe-making industries retail various replacement spikes. These "soft" spikes are nubs fitted to the bottom of the shoe, providing all the stability needed while sparing the course from too much damage.

As in all areas of sport, shoe-making has improved drastically over the last couple of decades and golfers can benefit greatly from these advances. For comfort, gel insoles that mold themselves to the shape of the golfer's foot are recommended and, while water-resistant outsoles are generally standard, it is worth remembering to check with the vendor.

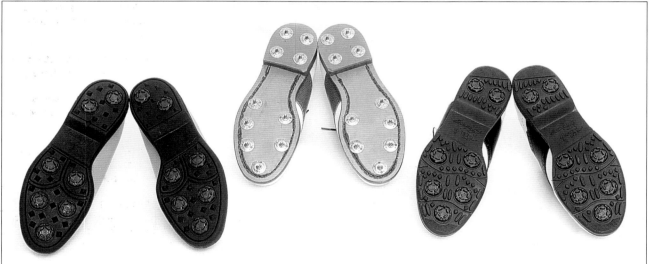

GLOVES

Again, modern gloves are wonders of technology. Synthetic materials are lightweight, thin, and durable—perfect for the feel required by golfers. The added bonuses of today's gloves include sections of mesh, which allow greater breathability, and hence more comfort. However, if you wish to treat yourself the cabretta leather of South American hairsheep, originally used to make top-of-the-range golfing gloves, is wonderfully luxurious.

ABOVE: Steel spikes are becoming a thing of the past.

ABOVE LEFT: Soft or plastic spikes are preferable as they do less damage to the green.

LEFT: Gloves are available in both leather and synthetic materials.

FAR LEFT: Gloves are designed to stretch where necessary.

OPPOSITE TOP: Golf shoes provide improved traction on the course.

OPPOSITE CENTER: Shoes are available in synthetic and leather materials.

OPPOSITE BOTTOM: Whatever your preference, shoes come in all colors and designs.

GOLF BAGS

A good bag should be lightweight and functional, furnished with plenty of convenient pockets and have a well-designed carry strap that distributes the weight of the bag evenly. Another feature that some bags now have, and which can be very useful if you're not blessed with the services of a caddy, is an automatic stand that pops up when the bag is set on the ground. Bags are available in an astonishing variety of colors and styles, so take your time choosing one that is right for you.

ABOVE: A useful addition to the golf bag design is a stand.

RIGHT: Special bags designed specifically for golf carts with all the pockets at the front or side make access easier.

OPPOSITE: Bags designed for easier carrying make walking around the golf course more enjoyable.

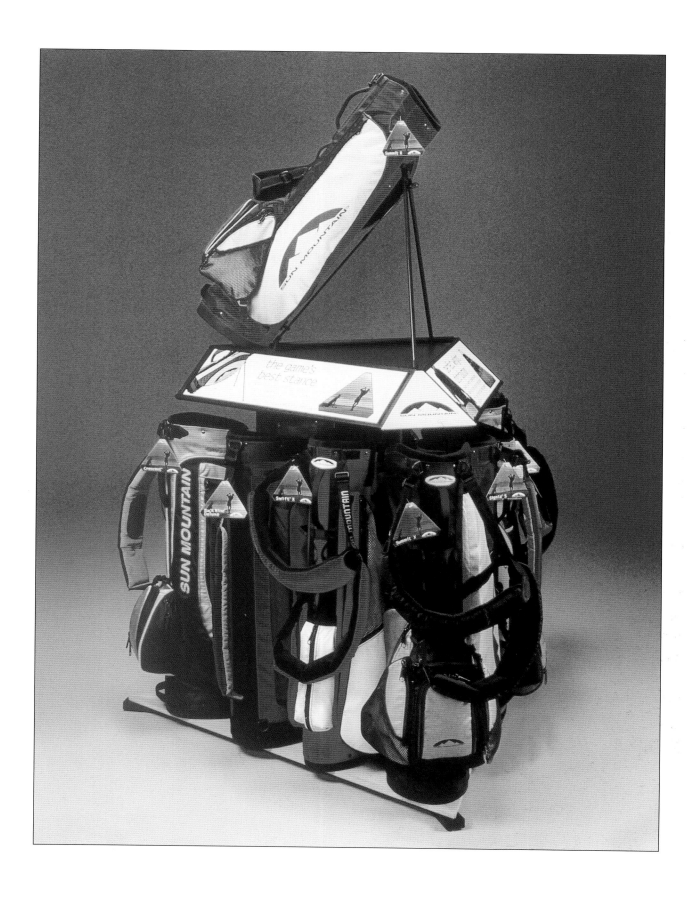

OTHER ACCESSORIES & TOOLS

These days there seems to be no end to the range of goods marketed for the golfing enthusiast. For those that can afford it a golf cart can ease the strain of lugging around 30 pounds of equipment. If you wish to stroll but still want to get rid of the cumbersome bag modern variations include electronic trollies that automatically follow a clip worn by the golfer. The trolley rolls while the golfer walks, and stops when the golfer does.

RIGHT: Electric golf carts are popular and are certainly beneficial to golfers who would not be able to play if walking were the only choice.

RIGHT: For those who like to walk without a bag this electric cart is the answer.

Another piece of technological wizardry for those who need to know the distance to their target is the yardage meter. These bounce an infrared beam off a faraway target and provide an exact distance.

Less costly, and more essential to the considerate golfer are divot repair tools. Small steel or plastic devices are sold for precisely this task and often are equipped with magnetic ball markers.

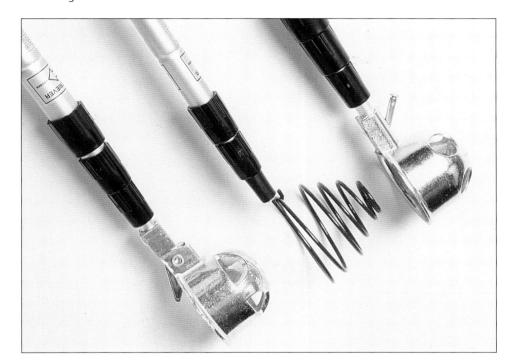

LEFT: Ball retrievers help golfers to fish their ball from water hazards and difficult places.

LEFT: Modern golf carts have a GPS system to help determine the distance to the flag, making club selection easier.

TEACHING AIDS

There are literally hundreds of teaching aids on the market, all designed to help the golfer achieve the correct positions in the golf swing. Anyone who's seen the movie *Tin Cup* will understand to what lengths the golfers will go to help their golf swing. Listed here are some of the most helpful teaching aids.

RIGHT: A student uses a teaching aid under the watchful eye of an instructor.

1.

2.

ELBOW TAC-TIC: As the collapsing of the left arm (for right handed golfers) is one of the most common faults (1), this teaching aid is especially useful. It has a hard plastic spine running down its length. If the arm bends it gives a loud clicking sound letting the golfer know when and where the arm is collapsing. The helps to make sure that the left arm stays straight ensuring solid contact with the ball (2).

3.

4.

Another use for the Elbow Tac-tic is to ensure a good extension of the left arm on the backswing (3). As a golfer's eyes are focused on the ball, he does not know if he is collapsing the left arm or not. Again, if the arm bends a clicking sound will be heard and gives the golfer the necessary feedback for helping keep the arm straight (4).

WRIST TAC-TIC: Made by the same company that makes the Elbow Tac-Tic, the Wrist Tac-Tic can be used for chipping and putting where there is a tendency for the left wrist to break down (5). Again, a plastic strip is built into it and a loud click is heard if the motion is not performed correctly. This gives the golfer that all important feedback necessary for producing a good consistent chipping and putting motion (6,7).

TOSKI'S TOUCH: Endorsed by teaching legend Bob Toski, this is another teaching aid that has many functions. It consists of a ball on a thin piece of rope with an attachment that can be applied to various parts of the body to achieve various functions.

Here it is strapped to the right knee (8) with the ball suspended just over the inside of the right foot. At the top of the backswing (9), the position is maintained, preventing the right hip from swaying back and the weight from going to the outside of the right foot, which are both undesirable positions. This ensures a good coil at the top of the backswing. The ball should finish on the outside of the left foot (10), indicating a good weight shift onto the front foot. The position of the ball at any given point in the swing tells the golfer whether he's executing it correctly or not.

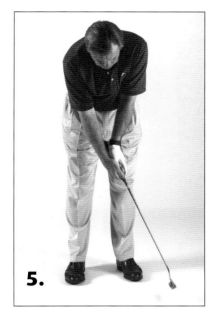

5.

6.

7.

8.

9.

10.

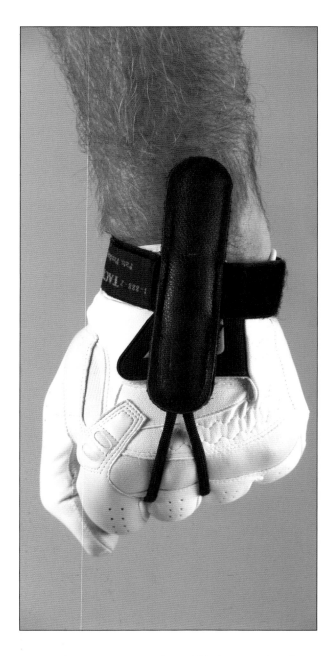

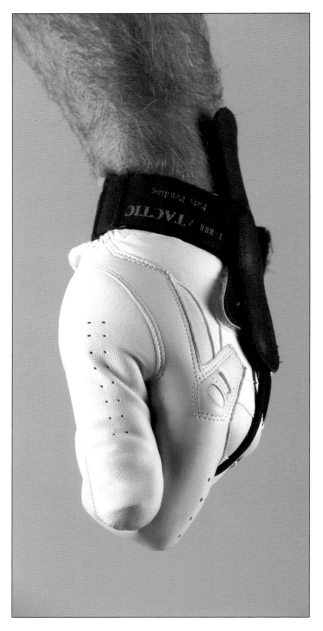

ABOVE: The Wrist Tac-Tic teaching aid helps remind students to keep the wrist flat, both in the short game (chipping) or the full swing (to prevent scooping).

TOP RIGHT: A practice putting cup can shoot the ball back to you so you only need to use one ball.

RIGHT: Plastic "whiffel" balls are another way to practice when space is limited.

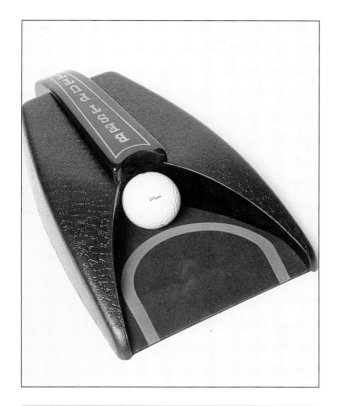

TOP: Extending an iron with another shaft gives feedback to the student if they are breaking down with their wrist.

ABOVE: A chipping net can be helpful to practice where space is a problem.

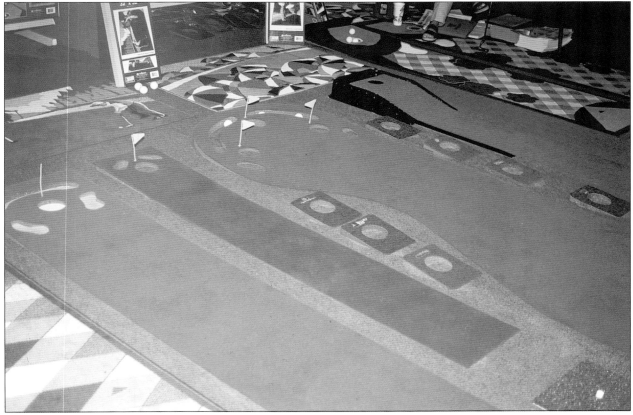

INSTRUCTIONAL VIDEOS

As with teaching aids, there are literally hundreds of instructional videos on the market. Some encompass all aspects of the game in one video, or with a series of tapes a different aspect is covered in each one.

If you are a visual learner then videotapes will definitely help your game. Instructional tapes by teaching professionals, who work with all levels of golfers day-to-day, are far more beneficial than those by "name" players. Tour players usually explain the way they play the game, which is on such a different level from the average golfer that it can be hard to relate to or imitate.

TOP LEFT: The Toski's Touch teaching aid has various uses from preventing swaying to helping weight shift.

TOP RIGHT: Practice nets that can be set up in a basement or backyard are useful if you do not live close to a driving range or course.

LEFT: Putting mats are a great way to practice your putting at home.

ABOVE: An example of some of the videos on the market. There are many alternatives available.

THE VALUE OF TAKING LESSONS

The best advice for anyone who is serious about improving their game is to take lessons. You'll be amazed at the difference in your game, your on-course attitude and the lower scores at the end of your rounds.

MAXIMIZING LESSONS

To get the best results don't arrive for the lesson wanting to cover everything and expecting a miracle. It is best to focus on one issue per lesson, master it, and move on. Give the instructor specific information where possible, such as "my drives are going right" or" my pitch shots are always short."

Arrive early to hit balls and warm up a little. Ask questions and make sure you get full explanations. You should receive homework in the form of drills. Immediately following the lesson take time to review the experience, take notes on key points to reinforce what was stressed in your video analysis session and perform the provided drills.

For approximately two weeks before your next lesson practice your drills and review your videotape. Make sure the teacher gives you some "at home" drills, such as swinging in front of a mirror and chipping and putting in your yard or on your rug for days when you can't get to the range. If a student is unwilling to work and practice between lessons, then lessons are not really very beneficial.

THE VALUE OF GOLF SCHOOLS

Private lessons with a local professional who knows your swing is a good way to keep up with the game over a long period of time. To accelerate the learning process for any skill level a golf school experience is ideal. It allows students to leave the stresses of home and work in a specialized atmosphere with real commitment to their goals. A three-day school allows students to work on the total game rather than just on one aspect of it.

CHOOSING A GOLF SCHOOL

Just as interest in the game of golf has grown, so have the number of golf schools and teaching approaches. Golf schools have become as much a part of the game as equipment. And the truth is that golfers can enjoy that valuable equipment a lot more if they use it in the right way.

Finding a school is easy. Choosing the right one for you is a little more difficult. You need to investigate the quality of instructors, teaching philosophy, size of the classes and the available facilities as well as the cost. Ask who the school's instructors are and how much teaching experience they have. Professional teachers ideally have several years of full-time instruction. They should also be specifically trained in the teaching methods advocated by the founders of the school. They must possess the ability to quickly analyze your individual need for improvement. It is crucial that the teachers are skilled in communicating simply and effectively with every level of golfer.

RIGHT: Taking instruction is a must for every golfer who wants to improve.

The size of classes at the school is very important. The best instruction comes with a low student to teacher ratio. It is not ideal to be placed in a large class with several instructors running about trying to relate to everyone in the same way at the same skill level. Each golfer has different strengths and weaknesses and needs individual attention.

There should be no more than four people in a class and one instructor should work with the same class throughout the entire program. In that way, the instructor gets to know each student's needs very well and the student receives continuity and rapport, which is very positive for the goal of improvement. Small classes assure flexibility of instruction, if one thing isn't working there are alternative ways to reach the student.

You'll want to know if the school's philosophy is geared towards building upon the strengths of the experienced golfers existing swing or geared towards rebuilding the swing from scratch. Does the school instruct on all aspects of the game or just on short game? Does the school help you with your mental approach to golf as well as physical? Good teaching pros acknowledge the importance of the mental side of golf but few schools devote the time for addressing mental preparation for the game.

Technology is also an important consideration in selecting a school. Computerized video analysis helps you monitor your progress while you are attending school. Then a personal take home videotape with a "voice-over" reinforces lessons when you return home.

ABOVE RIGHT: Mel shows a student the error of his ways.

RIGHT: Mel shows the student what he needs to do to correct his problem. In this case increasing the backswing arc.

A golf school facility should have a private driving range, bunkers, chipping, pitching, and putting areas. Classrooms for private video analysis are important. Unlimited range ball should be provided for practice after school. An 18-hole golf course as part of the school's complex lets you put what you've learned to the test. If accommodations and meals are needed ask what is available on site or nearby.

Follow-up to ensure continued and lasting improvement is important when school is finished. The following three methods may be offered by some golf schools:

1. **GAME ANALYSIS:** Your golf school may provide a game analysis system, where for example you can post your scores after each round and create statistical categories for you to see the strengths and weaknesses of your game. Common categories are fairways hit, greens in regulation, and number of putts. Your instructor can use this information to monitor your progress and give you advice and analysis as you continue to improve.

2. **VIDEO ANALYSIS:** Some schools offer to review your swing by videotape. An instructor can compare your swings to those made while you were at school and offer analysis or prescribe drills.

3. **E-MAIL:** Students may be offered the option of e-mailing any questions, comments, and improvement status. Many students find this a simple and cost-effective way to get a quick tip and to inform of their progress.

Finally, is the school highly rated by reputable golf magazines and other media? *Golf Magazine*, for example, issues a biennial ranking of the top 25 Golf Schools in America. The rankings are derived from the magazine's critique on the quality of teachers, programs and facilities and also from thousands of golf school graduates who were surveyed to rate their experiences. If a school is consistently ranked in this way, feel confident about enrolling.

STRETCHING, EXERCISING, AND WARMING UP

Exercises that maintain or increase flexibility, build strength, and help you warm up are greatly beneficial to any game of golf. However, do not follow any of the exercises if you have any doubts about your ability to complete them effectively. Check with your physician before starting if necessary.

STRETCHES FOR FLEXIBILITY

1.

2.

3.

No matter what age you are, flexibility is a definite requirement for a good golf swing. As you get older you need to retain that flexibility. In this first exercise, have the club above your head (1). Gently lean over to the right as far as you can go (2). Repeat to the other side (3). Do this exercise four or five times, gently.

4.

To do this exercise correctly make sure you maintain a straight spine. Place the shaft across your shoulders (4). Get into your golf posture and gently twist until you have made a full shoulder turn (5). Repeat to the other side (6).

5.

6.

Avoid moving your torso up and down in order to maintain the correct angle for your spine. The pictures here (7,8, & 9) show the incorrect way to do the exercise.

8.

7.

9.

If holding the club on your shoulders is too difficult for you, put the club into the small of your back and hook your arms around the club (10). Gently twist in this position to achieve a full shoulder turn on each side (11 & 12).

To stretch underneath your arm, take the palm of your right hand and put it on the elbow of your left arm, which is stretched above you. Gently pull the right hand toward the right shoulder until you feel a gentle stretch (13). Do the same with the other arm (14). Repeat four or five times.

To increase flexibility in the upper shoulder area, take a long club such as a driver and hold it in your right hand with the shaft going behind the arm (15). Very gently pull the lower part of the driver forward, stretching the upper part of the arm (16). Repeat with the left arm. This is particularly for the right arm

(for right-handed golfers) as it helps you to get into the "tray" position mentioned later in this book. It is very important to do this exercise gently so that you do not pull any muscles.

A gentle stretch, such as this, for two or three minutes per day will be extremely beneficial for loosening the shoulders and upper arms.

Finally sit on the ground with your right leg crossed over your outstretched left leg (17). Gently push the back of your left arm against the right knee until you feel a gentle stretch in your lower back. Repeat on this side for three or four times before changing to the other leg (18).

Do not do any of these exercises if you have serious back problems and may pull a muscle or have any other health concerns. If in doubt please ask your doctor for advice.

10.

11.

12.

13.

14.

15.

16.

17.

18.

EXERCISES FOR STRENGTH

Additional exercises to increase strength in the muscles directly involved in the golf swing will help you hit the ball further and improve endurance for better play on a full 18-hole golf course.

The equipment illustrated here is called a "Home Gym" and is endorsed by world champion golfer and exercise fanatic Gary Player. It consists of a grip attached to some rubber tubing that you can attach to a door handle or doorjamb and makes exercising at home a fairly simple task.

The equipment is not bulky and can be stored away in a draw and retrieved for your next workout without much effort. Purchasing some strong rubber tubing from a medical supply store would work equally as well as a substitute.

In the first exercise, attach the elastic cord to the top of the door and hold the grip only with your left hand (1) before slowly pulling it down (2). Maintain the stiffness of your left arm and allow the forearm to rotate to simulate the impact position. The back of your left hand is where it should be at impact during

1.

2.

a full swing. This exercise is great for feeling how the left forearm should move on the downswing. It also strengthens the shoulder and tricep muscles of the left arm. Return slowly to your initial position (1). Do between five and ten repetitions depending on how strong you are.

In the second exercise, hold the grip with both hands as you would a golf club (3), and pull down gently to an extension position (4). During this exercise you can definitely feel the role the left side plays in generating power in the golf swing. Maintain the straightness of the left arm, but feel the right arm extending fully and rotating slightly over the left, duplicating the post impact position. At this point the weight should primarily be on the left side. In this exercise you'll be strengthening not only the muscles in the left arm but the shoulder, forearm and tricep muscles of the right arm. Do between five and ten repetitions depending on your strength.

3.

4.

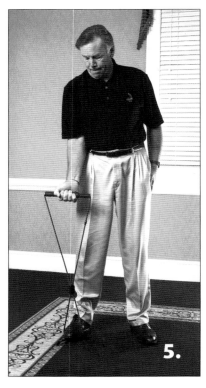

5.

6.

For a bicep curl, the rubber cord is attached to your right foot and your right hand holds the grip with the palm upward (5). Pull the right forearm until your hand touches your right shoulder (6). Do between five and ten repetitions depending on your strength, and then change to the other foot and the other arm for the same routine.

Attach the cord to your right foot and take your normal golfing grip and stance. Now extend both your left and right arms directly down in front of you maintaining the straightness of your left arm (7) and then allow the right forearm to cross over the left (8). This duplicates the motion of a good extension and rotation through the ball and you're working all the muscles in the hands, wrists, forearms, and shoulders. Allow your left hip to clear slightly but maintain your spine angle and do not straighten up. Do between five and ten repetitions depending on your strength.

7.

8.

9.

10.

Attach the rubber cord to a door handle and hold the grip with your right hand, palm facing forward and right elbow close to your side (9). Pull your right forearm slowly forward until your right hand is touching your left hip (10). This strengthens the wrist and forearm and also the rotator-cuff area of the right arm. Do between five and ten repetitions depending on your strength.

11.

12.

This exercise is similar to that above, but uses the left arm. Hold the grip with your left hand, palm facing inward (11) and pull your left forearm slowly forward until the palm is facing outward (12).

Make sure the upper arm stays close to your side and the forearm stays parallel to the ground throughout the entire motion. Do between five and ten repetitions depending on your strength.

WARMING UP

In order to play well consistently, warming up before you tee off is important. Play starts on the very first hole, so be ready to play on the first tee. In order to do that, warm up on the practice tee first. Starting with your pitching wedge, slowly graduate upward with the even-numbered clubs all the way up to the driver. Don't hit more than five or six balls with each of the clubs.

Now work back down with the odd clubs, finishing your range work with a few pitches, and then head over to the putting green. Hit a few long putts to develop feel for the day and finally finish by working on some three-footers before heading to the first tee. Warming up before a round should be just that; do not use this time to try and "fix" an ailing swing. You are not going to find a miracle cure thirty minutes before you tee off. Instead, focus on rhythm and balance and you will be pleasantly surprised how effortless the swing feels. Take that rhythmical swing onto the course for a better and more consistent round. If you do happen to play poorly, go to the practice tee immediately after the round, because you still have the feel of what you were doing and can take steps to remedy the situation.

If you do not have time to practice immediately after the round, see your teaching professional before your next round to work out the kinks. Maybe forfeit the next round of golf to put in some extra practice time. This will pay dividends and your next round will be much more enjoyable.

For those of you who arrive at the golf course just in time for your tee-time, here are a few additional warm-up exercises you can do on the first tee. Take your pitching wedge and sand wedge (the two heaviest clubs in the bag) and swing them gently back and forth, slowly increasing the length of the swing until you finally reach full swing length (1&2).

1.

Cross your right foot over your left and gently lean forward letting your arms hang relaxed (3). Slowly increase your bend from the waist to stretch out your hamstrings. Do this for approximately 30 seconds. Then cross your left foot over your right and repeat the same exercise.

This brief routine will stretch and warm up your muscles and help you get your round off to a good start.

2.

3.

STARTING OUT

Whether you're a beginner just starting out or an experienced golfer it is important to spend some time working on your game. The question often asked is how much time should be spent practicing and how much time should be spent playing on the course? It depends on exactly what you want out of this wonderful game. If you have aspirations of becoming a good golfer, then hard work on the practice tee along with some good instruction is a must. Spend some time on the range before you tee off, starting with the short irons (1&2) and

gradually work up to the woods, focusing mainly on rhythm and balance (3, 4 & 5). However, if you want to play this game just for fun, then by all means go out with your friends and don't worry about your score. Although, to have fun on the golf course, you need to have some level of ability so some instruction and practice would still be required.

When you do practice, work on all aspects of the game. Spend 50 percent of your practice time on pitching, chipping, bunker shots, and putting; 25 percent working on your irons; and 25 percent working on your fairway woods and driver.

PRACTICING AT HOME

For those of you who have busy lives, hectic careers, and families to take care of, it is not always easy to find time to head to the course or practice range. There are many shots you can practice at home that only take a few minutes a day. The most obvious one is putting. You can work on your putting stroke on your carpet, using a ruler to check your putterhead path (1 to 7 overleaf). You can also practice chipping to a small target, such as a coin or tee, in the yard.

One of the most beneficial things to practice at home is swinging a club out-doors, focusing on technique (as seen in 1 to 12 on this page and overleaf). Early in my golf career, I would get home from school, grab a club, and stand and swing in the backyard for hours. This practice kept my golfing muscles limber, so when I went to the golf course on the weekend my body was comfortable with my swing and I

was able to improve fairly quickly. I recommend every beginning golfer go through this routine on a regular basis and improvement will be far more rapid.

Ask at your club or the course that you play, about who has a good reputation as an instructor in your area. Depending on your goals, set up a series of lessons, or go to a golf school to get a solid foundation.

Reading books and magazines on golf can be beneficial. However, the golfer should be selective in deciding which tips to incorporate into their swing, and which tips to stay away from. As the novice golfer can misinterpret the written word on golf tips, consult your teaching pro for clarity and to decide if a given tip will benefit you personally.

THE GRIP

The most neglected element of the golf swing is the grip. Bad grips are more common than bad swings, and a good player is never seen with a bad grip. The problem begins when the student is unsure which of the three grips is best. It depends on your body type. Do you have strong hands and arms, are you weak in that area, or are your fingers long and thin or short and pudgy? This will determine the right grip for you. For reasons of clarity "top hand" and "bottom hand" will be used rather than "left" or "right" for the benefit of left- as well as right-handed golfers.

THE BASEBALL GRIP

The baseball or ten finger grip is good for female and senior golfers who do not have a lot of strength in their wrists and forearms. This allows the lower hand to be a little more active through the hitting area helping rotation to square the clubface, resulting in straighter shots and more distance (1).

THE OVERLAPPING GRIP

The overlapping or Vardon grip (after Harry Vardon) is the most popular. It is suitable for most male and female golfers with strong arms and wrists and unifies the hands, helping them work as one unit (2).

THE INTERLOCKING GRIP

The interlocking grip works well for people with short fingers and pudgy palms, who find it difficult to get the small finger to overlap. The small finger of the upper hand and the index finger of the lower hand interlock, unifying the hands, and allowing them to work as one unit (3). (Jack Nicklaus uses this grip.)

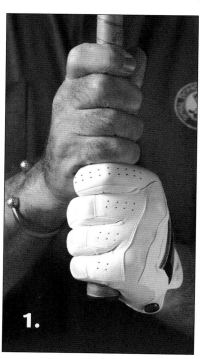

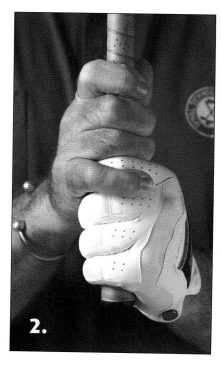

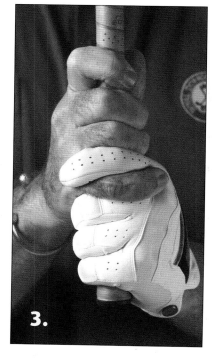

THE TOP HAND POSITION

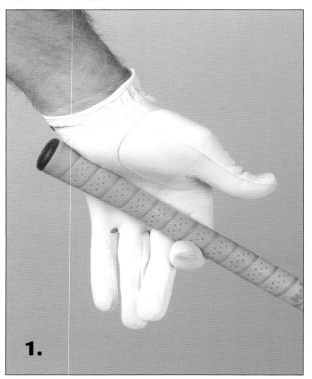

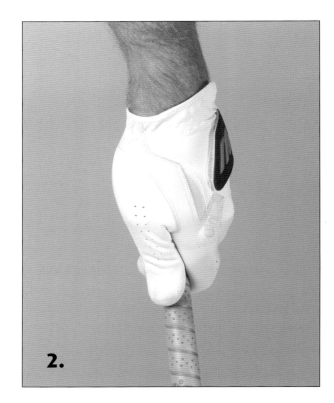

THE BOTTOM HAND POSITION

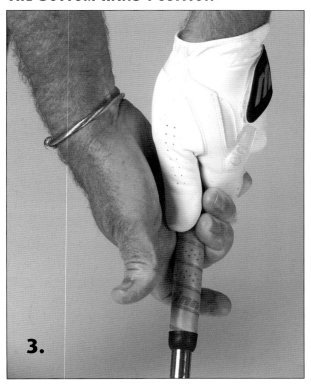

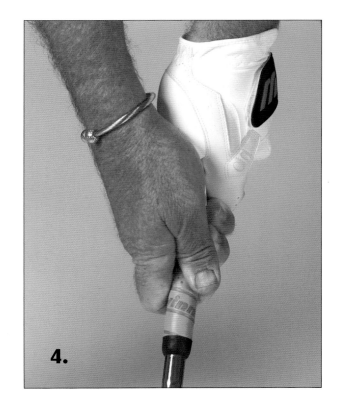

There are a number of common requisites regardless of which grip you choose.

THE TOP HAND POSITION

The top hand needs to be placed on the club so that looking down at your hands you can see two knuckles (1 & 2). The line formed by the thumb and the back of the hand must point to the right shoulder (left shoulder for left-handers).

THE BOTTOM HAND POSITION

The bottom hand is placed on the club with the palms adjacent to one another and the lines formed by the thumbs and the back of the hands are parallel to one another. The lifeline of the bottom hand fits snugly over the thumb of the top hand. The thumb and index finger of the bottom hand form a slight "trigger grip" and the tips of each finger touch (3 & 4).

AIMING THE CLUB

More faults in the golf swing are associated with poor alignment than any other cause. Golfers are often unaware of lining up incorrectly, so problems such as pulling, pushing, and slicing ensue.

Obviously if you do not line yourself up correctly it is very difficult to hit the ball straight on a consistent basis. Aiming your clubface to the target is critical. Take the scenario of a golfer with a good golf swing who unknowingly aims slightly to the right of his target. He makes a perfect swing and the ball misses his target to the right. He automatically assumes that he has made a poor swing, and when lining up to the next shot, tries to correct the fault by pulling the ball back online. An "over the top" swing now starts to develop, where the clubhead path cuts across the ball and soon this good golf swing has lost

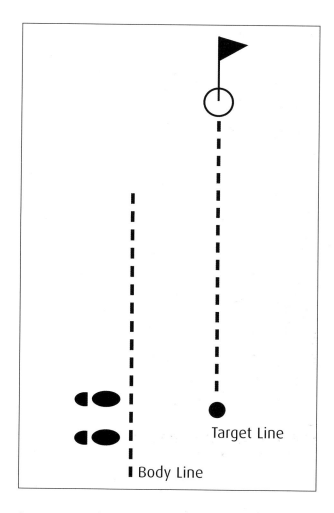

Target Line

Body Line

its power and direction. As these problems persist the golfer continually tries to correct them by correcting a fault with a fault. The first thing that needs to be corrected is alignment. Pay attention to your own alignment and never hit a shot while you are lined up incorrectly.

Whether hitting a drive, iron shot, fairway wood, or a putt the alignment procedure is the same. There are two lines associated with aiming, the target line, a line drawn from the ball to the target, and the body line, a line drawn through the toes parallel to the target line. In fact your toes, hips, and shoulders are aiming slightly left of the target in order to have the clubface perfectly aligned to the target (see diagram above).

On the practice tee, always place a club down on the ground to help you with alignment and to prevent poor swing habits from developing because of bad alignment. Golfers can get so wrapped up working on their swing mechanics that they totally forget about alignment. Never start a practice session without a specific target, particularly when working on your full swing. By always using a club for alignment during a practice session, you get used to lining up correctly, and this will carry over to the golf course. You can also incorporate alignment into your pre-shot routine (see pages 72–73).

LEFT: This range has 2x4in white wooden boards separating the golfers which can be used to help with alignment.

STANCE

The stance should be about as wide as the shoulders for all clubs when you are using a full swing. As there is only one golf swing for all standard full shots, use the same width stance regardless of whether you are hitting a driver or an iron.

The back foot should be set at 90 degrees to the target line, and the front foot turned out about 30 degrees. By squaring off the back foot it creates a stable back leg and prevents swaying. By toeing the front foot out slightly, you are able to clear your body easier on the downswing.

The only time you should widen your stance is on a windy day to prevent the wind from blowing you off balance. Your weight should be distributed evenly between the heels and toes of both feet, with the weight slightly on the inside of both feet at the address position (see below).

1.

2.

SQUARE STANCE

A square stance occurs when both feet are positioned along the body line and square to the target line (1). The knees, hips and shoulders should also be square to this line. This stance should be used most of the time.

OPEN STANCE

An open stance has the front foot pulled slightly back from the body line (2). This stance allows the hips to clear quicker on the downswing and will promote a slight outside-in swing which will produce a fade. The knees, hips, and shoulders are pointing slightly left of the target line.

CLOSED STANCE

A closed stance occurs when the back foot is pulled slightly back from the body line (3). This stance allows the hips to rotate a little more in the backswing and promotes a slightly bigger shoulder turn. It also helps to produce a draw. The knees, hips, and shoulders are pointing slightly right of the target line.

3.

THE ADDRESS POSITION

For reasons of clarity for both left- and right-handed golfers, the terms "front" and "back" rather than "left" or "right" are used here. For example, the front foot would be the left foot for right-handers.

SETUP:

WIDTH OF STANCE

The stance should be approximately the width of the shoulders for the mid-irons (1), slightly narrower for the shorter clubs, and slightly wider for the longer clubs (with emphasis on the word "slightly"). The back foot should be set at 90 degrees to your target line in order to prevent the hip from sliding laterally on the backswing. The front foot should be turned out slightly in order to facilitate the clearing of the front side on the downswing.

2.

1.

HAND POSITION

This is an often neglected position at address. It is important that there is a straight line from the top of the front shoulder to the ball (2). This sets the hands in the correct position relative to the ball position. Note that the butt of the club should be over the middle of the front thigh regardless of which club is in your hand.

POSTURE

Only slightly bend your knees (too much bend causes all sorts of problems with the backswing). Your arms should hang down vertically from the shoulders (2). This helps keep any tension out of the arms at the address position. Tension in the arms at address also causes problems on the backswing. The spine should be relatively straight and the chin held slightly away from the chest.

3.

4.

5.

BALL POSITION:
THE IRONS

The ball position for all regular iron shots (not low/high/uphill/downhill lies) is about 2in inside the front heel. This automatically sets the hands slightly ahead of the ball and helps give the desired "slightly downward" blow that is required for crisp iron shots (3).

THE FAIRWAY WOODS

The ball position for the fairway woods is directly off the left heel. This automatically sets the hands even with the ball and helps give the desired "bottom of the arc" blow required for lofted fairways shots (4).

THE DRIVE

The ball position for the driver is off the instep of the front foot. This automatically sets the hands even with the clubhead and helps give the desired "slightly upward" blow required for good tee shots (5).

PRE-SHOT ROUTINE

The next time you watch golf on TV notice what the players do before they play each shot. Each one of them goes through their "pre-shot routine" which will be exactly the same each time. Many students of golf say that they would like to be more consistent, and this is one way to ensure that. Each pro has his or her own pre-shot routine and you will probably want to develop your own.

Two elements that should be included in the routine are visualization and alignment.

Take your first practice swing next to the ball (1). (Some players prefer to take their practice swing behind the ball, which is fine as well.)

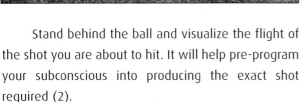

Stand behind the ball and visualize the flight of the shot you are about to hit. It will help pre-program your subconscious into producing the exact shot required (2).

Once that is done pick a spot about 2ft in front of your ball but on line with your target, walk around and align the clubface to that spot (3). It is much easier to line up to something close to you rather that a long way off, so pick an "intermediate" target. Go into the address position and hit your shot (4).

A pre-shot routine will not only help with consistency but the visualization will improve your overall game. The key point to remember is, do the same thing each time and don't vary your routine at any time in order to maintain consistency.

THE SWING

Having taught many golfers for many years, one question is asked more than any other: Once I'm in my address position, what is the correct way to start the swing?

Much has been written about the takeaway, such as take it back with the left side or the right side, use the arms to take it back, the big muscles, or the hands. There isn't any particular way to take the club back in terms of how it feels, only in terms of where the club should be at particular times during the swing. Although we may all have the same bone and muscle structure, we have different perceptions on how things feel. The only instruction that can be given is to indicate where the club should be at each point on the swing. When the student is in the correct position, only he or she know how it feels for them and how best to achieve it.

THE BACKSWING

In Starting Out (pages 56–73) the target line and body line is mentioned in relation to the address position. At the start of the takeaway, you want the hands to move straight back along the body line with no manipulation or rotation of the hands or arms. In other words, the hands are passive and the torso rotates.

Halfway up the backswing the club position should appear as in 1 and 2. As you can see, the clubhead is still slightly outside the body line. It is important not confuse this statement to mean the clubhead is outside the target line. (If the club moved straight back the arms would pull away from the body.) Most good players today have the club in this position, including Nicklaus, Couples, and Els, among others.

What you do not want is for the club to get behind you or to get too much on the inside as this causes the wrists to rotate laying the clubface open. This ultimately lays the club off (pointing to the left for right-handed golfers) at the top of the backswing, a sure way of starting the downswing "over the top."

If the grip pressure is light at this point the wrists will start to "cock" naturally with the momentum of the clubhead and the club will start

1.

2.

3.

4.

to break upwards. At this stage the hands are approximately in the middle of the chest and the club will feel very light in your hands (3&4).

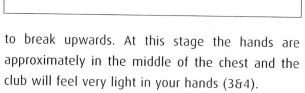

Continue with a full shoulder turn to the top of the backswing (5&6).

OTHER POINTS TO NOTE ON THE BACKSWING

The right knee does not move from its original position, all the way to the top of the swing. This stable position ensures that the proper "torque" is created in the body.

The left arm stays reasonably straight, not rigid, throughout the backswing, especially at the top of the swing, a definite problem area for a lot of golfers. If the left arm breaks down you will again lose that necessary "torque" that produces the necessary power on the downswing.

The weight moves over to the right side at the top of the backswing with the sternum directly over the right foot. This prevents a "reverse pivot," ensuring the proper weight shift and making the start of the downswing a lot easier and more powerful.

5.

6.

SWING PLANE

There are two swing planes to be aware of, the shaft plane and the arm plane:

THE SHAFT PLANE

Halfway up the backswing the shaft should be either pointing at the ball or slightly inside the ball (1). You definitely do not want the shaft pointing outside the ball line (2). This is called "laying the club off."

THE ARM PLANE

The arm plane is a line drawn at address from the ball through the shoulders and extending upwards. At the top of the backswing the left arm should be on this line (3).

Making both of these moves will ensure you are swinging the club "on plane." Practice these moves in front of a mirror in order to both see and feel the correct positions, so that when you go to the practice tee you'll know what to strive for.

THE DOWNSWING

Starting from the top of the backswing, the first move of the downswing starts with the left side (for right-handed golfers). It does not start with the arms, as is so commonly seen among high and medium handicap golfers.

Note that the weight has started to shift across to the front side and the angle created by the shaft and the left arm has not changed. This indicates that the downswing has not been started with the hands.

Any attempt to start the downswing with the hands and arms will immediately cause two things to happen. One, you will "come over the top" and two, you will instantly lose that all important shaft angle and get what is called "casting" because it is like casting a fishing rod. This means instant power loss, and directional loss as well. In picture 2 the hands have already passed hip level and the angle created by the shaft and left arm is still the same as it was at the top of the backswing. The weight is now approximately 60 percent across onto the front side.

The all important "impact" position is shown in picture 3. If you compare 2 with 3 you can see that the hands have moved approximately 12in in the same time that the clubhead has moved 5ft, obviously creating tremendous clubhead speed. At impact your weight should be approximately 70 percent over to the front side and the left arm and shaft are in a straight line. At this moment all the power that has been stored up during the downswing is being released at the correct point, at impact.

Any golfer wanting to improve his or her distance has only to look to these areas to see where the power is being lost. A lesson with the use of a video camera will quickly illustrate this. Once you understand the principals involved in creating "the power move" you will be pleased to see your distance increase and your score come down.

1.

2.

3.

INCORRECT POSITION OF THE FOREARM

FAULT: Most golfers allow the right forearm to get out of "perpendicular" too soon on the downswing (right). This causes the hands to get too far away from the body, which in turn will cause you to cut across the ball, causing a slice or a pull depending on where the clubface is at impact.

CURE: From the top of the backswing (1), drop the right arm down so that the forearm is still pointing directly behind you halfway down the downswing (2). The hands should stay close to the body until just before impact. This will produce an inside-out clubhead path, allowing the clubhead to travel down the line towards the target (3).

1.

2.

3.

THE FOLLOW-THROUGH

Why worry about the follow-through? The ball is gone and it will not make any difference. However, a good follow-through can help you to get better scores.

You can learn a lot by being aware of your position at the end of your swing. Watch the touring pros after they hit a shot during competition. They hold their follow-through position as they watch the flight of the ball. Their balance is good and all of their weight is on their front leg. In fact they can lift the back foot and still keep their balance.

All the weight in picture 1 is on the front foot and the arms have completed their momentum over the shoulder. The back foot is right up on the toe and the sole of the back shoe (2) is visible. This is the ideal position for the follow-through.

The follow-through is mainly the result of what has gone before. In other words, the backswing is the setup of the swing, the downswing is creating the power and the follow-through will indicate what transpired during those phases. During your practice sessions hold your position at the end of the swing and try to feel where you are.

Following are some of the things to look for and how to correct them.

1.

2.

Is all your weight on the front foot or do you still have some weight on the back? If so, work on improving your weight shift by starting the downswing with a lateral slide of the hips, moving the weight from your back foot (3) to your front foot (4) before the clubhead gets to the ball. If you have done this correctly there will be no weight on your back foot at the end of your swing.

3.

4.

Are your hands finishing low across the front of your body as in picture 5? This is usually caused by spinning the hips right from the top of your back-swing, causing the clubhead to cut across the ball and your hands to finish below the shoulder. Start the downswing by transferring your weight to your front foot with a lateral movement of the hips, allowing you to keep the clubhead on line to your target (6) which will allow you to finish in a bal-anced position with your hands above and over your shoulder (7).

5.

6.

7.

8.

9.

Are your hands finishing just in front of your body (8) instead of following right through (9)? This is an indication of not clearing the left hip fast enough as you swing through the ball. This will almost certainly cause a lack of power or loss in distance. Most students who finish in this position are those who like to play a lot but do not put in the necessary time on the practice tee. They start steering the ball in order to keep the ball in play. To fully trust your swing on the course you must put the time in on the practice range making positive, aggressive swings.

10.

11.

If you are losing your balance forward (10), you are probably starting the downswing with your upper body instead of your legs. Again, weight shift, a good extension of the arms down the target line, and a complete body rotation is important, allowing the weight to move to the left heel with the belt buckle ending up facing the target (11).

In order to play good, consistent golf you have to put some time in on the practice range. This is where you can develop a sound, repetitive swing, not on the course. Remember to pay close attention to your follow-through in the future, it is more important than you think.

POSTURE

Incorrect posture will create many problems during both the backswing and the downswing. Spine angle is critical to hitting good golf shots, and if set in the wrong position at address, cannot be corrected during the swing.

FAULT: Poor posture at address, with the spine curved, the shoulders slumped.

FAULT: Poor posture at address, with knees stiff and arms extended outwards.

CURE: Take a club and put it behind your back with the shaft touching both your head and the base of your spine (1). Lean forward slightly from the waist, keeping the shaft in contact with your head and base of the spine (2). Remove the club, maintain this position, and place the club on the ground. This is the correct spine angle at address (3), and it will allow you to make a proper turn on the backswing. The knees are slightly flexed and the arms hang comfortably.

2.

1.

3.

DRILLS FOR MORE DISTANCE

We all seek more distance and manufacturers use this desire to sell us new equipment each year. However, good swing mechanics will help you develop more power than any new driver.

THE BASEBALL DRILL

Take your driver and holding it out in front of you, make a turn horizontally as if you were swinging a baseball bat (1). Now swing through as hard as you can, trying to make the "whoosh" happen beyond the "front" of your body (2). In other words the "whoosh" happens beyond where you started the club. In order to do this correctly you have to use your body and not your arms. Once you have this feeling of creating power with your torso, go back to your regular stance and try to duplicate the same feeling. You'll hear the "whoosh" after impact, telling you that you have reached maximum clubhead speed at impact, definitely resulting in more distance.

1.

2.

THE "WHOOSH DRILL"

If you have a problem creating the "whoosh" described in the previous drill, flip the club over and hold the club by the head (3). Again swing the club trying to create the "whoosh" after the impact position (4). You will discover that you can only do this if you turn the body ahead of the arms. Recreate this feeling with the club the right way round and you will start seeing your drives fly further!

3.

4.

5.

INCREASING THE WIDTH OF YOUR ARC DRILL

The bigger your arc on the backswing the more club-head speed you will produce on the downswing. However, most golfers think they are creating a wide arc when in fact they are not. Test yourself in the following manner to see if you are taking the club back as wide as you can.

Put your headcover behind the head of your driver (5) and as you start your backswing (6), push the headcover straight back. If you can push the headcover beyond your right foot you are taking the club back correctly. If not, you are picking your club up too quickly with your hands (7).

6.

7.

FAIRWAY WOODS

Golfers have trouble with fairway woods because they incorrectly judge the shot. Some treat the shot the same way as they would their driver, because it is a wood they think they should swing it in the same way.

Some try to lift the ball off the ground, either collapsing their left arm (for right-handed golfers) or straightening up in an effort to get the ball airborne. Both efforts result in either a topped shot, or hitting a ball without much height off the bottom of the club.

BALL POSITION

This is often the main culprit of poor fairway wood shots. Most golfers err in positioning the ball the same as with their driver. They place it off the instep of the front foot.

In the address position with a fairway wood (right), the ball position is directly opposite the left heel. With a normal golf swing this represents the bottom of the arc, which is exactly where to make contact with the ball.

Go ahead and swing, making sure you get the feeling of driving the ball forward and not up. This is accomplished by keeping the clubhead low and long through the hitting area (1). Make an aggressive swing through the ball, and try not to "steer" the ball down the fairway (2). Let the follow-through go right over your left shoulder (3).

If your fairway woods are a problem on the golf course, don't avoid them on the practice range but rather work on the correct technique to gain the

1.

confidence to hit the shots well. Once you start hitting your fairway woods well on the practice range you will have no problem carrying that swing over to the golf course.

2.

3.

WOODS VERSUS IRONS?

A frequently asked question is: "How do I adjust my swing for woods versus irons?

First of all, you do not want to "adjust" your swing or swing your woods differently from your irons. The swings are basically the same. The only difference is that the plane of the swing will be a little "flatter" with the woods than the irons due to the longer shaft.

The plane of the swing is a line drawn from the ball through the shoulders and extending on up (see the section on swing plane, page 79). At the top of the backswing, the back of the left hand (for right-handed golfers) should be on this line.

The swing plane appears more upright with the iron (1) than with a wood (2). Standing further away from the ball with the wood (2) the swing is automatically "flatter."

Most golfers will hit a 5 wood better than a 3 wood and a 3 wood better than a driver because of the loft of the club. A 5 wood will have more backspin and less sidespin than a 3 wood, and the same will apply with the 3 versus the driver. With the driver, there is minimum backspin, and even a slight error in clubface angle or clubhead path will result in sidespin and the greater the clubhead speed the more off-line the ball will travel. Even the touring pros will tend to tee off with a 3 wood when accuracy is more important than distance. Just watch the U.S. Open, where the rough is traditionally punishing—the pros will be teeing off with 3 woods and 2 irons quite often.

HOW TO SWING AT 90 PERCENT

Most amateurs know that 105 percent feeling, but here is a way to develop that Ernie Els or Freddie Couples "syrupy" swing.

Warm up at the range first. Then start hitting an 8 iron at your "flat out" 100 percent swing and mark down the yardage. Using an 8 iron as an example, you may hit 160 yards at 100 percent. Now divide that by two, and start hitting that same 8 iron to your new yardage. This now becomes your 50 percent swing, for example 80 yards. It is important to practice this swing in order to teach yourself the control you will need later. Now set a new target at 75 percent of your distance, for example 120 yards, and practice hitting this shot consistently to that target. This is now your 75 percent swing. See how easy it feels.

Finally, 90 percent of 160 yards is 144 yards and this is now the swing to use on the course. It is very macho to hit the 8 iron 160 yards, but your ball striking and accuracy will improve vastly without having to change anything major in your swing.

One of the other benefits of this 90 percent swing is that if you are between clubs, you can always go down one club and swing a little harder to get the desired distance. This gives you many more options on the course. If your iron shots are finding their target more often, you may want to do this drill with your driver to start hitting more fairways as well.

In pictures 1, 2, and 3 the takeaway is long slow and deliberate. In pictures 4, 5, and 6 (overleaf) the momentum of the club works upwards, the sign of good technique and a soft grip pressure. In pictures 7

7.

8.

9.

10.

to 10 the torso makes a complete turn and the left shoulder is under the chin. The weight has shifted to the front foot at the start of the downswing (11 & 12) and the club is "lagging" indicating that no attempt is made to hit with the arms. Pictures 13 and 14 show the end result of doing everything correctly. The club is working directly down the line to the target ensuring a straight shot. The swing comes to a full follow-through in pictures 15 & 16 with all the weight on the front foot and in good balance.

PITCHING

Most of the amateurs hit the ball well from tee to green, but when they get within 50 yards of the green they seem to struggle. "I don't have time to practice these shots," they say, "the pros have all the time in the world to stand and work on these shots, so they develop 'feel.' "

Here is a method that requires a little practice initially, but once you have established your distances, you will be able to rely on it in the future.

THE TECHNIQUE

The ball position is approximately 2in inside the left heel. The stance is slightly open, presetting the left hip in an open position which will allow you to clear the left side later on in the down-swing. Most of the weight is set forward on the left foot, which will push the hands slightly forward setting the shaft ahead of the ball (left). This allows for a slightly downward blow to create the height and backspin you need for this shot. The feet are fairly close together, allowing for an easier body rotation. If the feet are too wide apart, you will have trouble turning quickly enough through this shot.

THE 7-8-9 DISTANCE METHOD

Imagine as you address the ball that you have a large clock in front of you. Learn to swing your left arm (right arm for left handers) to the various "hours" of the clock.

In the 7-o'clock position (1), there is a slight wrist cock. This is important as you need to cock the wrist to help deliver a slightly downward blow through the shot. Practice hitting balls like this until you can consistently hit shots a certain distance. This will become your 7-o'clock shot.

In the 8-o'clock position (2), practice hitting balls in the same manner swinging your left arm to 8-o'clock and note your distances. This will become

your 8-o'clock shot. In the 9-o'clock position (3), practice the same technique as with the first two shots, while swinging your left arm to 9-o'clock. Finish off swinging the left arm to 10-o'clock (4) and you will now have four specific distances that you can consistently pitch the ball.

Distances will vary from player to player as in full shots, but once you have them established you have a tried and true method to rely on. When you find yourself 40 yards from the flag on the course you can say to yourself, "OK, this is my 9-o'clock shot," for example and you know for sure that if you swing your arm to that position, the ball is going to go about 40 yards.

1.

2.

3.

4.

KEY FEATURES OF PITCHING

At address the majority of your weight should be on your front foot (1). This keeps your body steady during the swing and helps you impart the downward blow important in creating the backspin you want on this shot. Note also looking at the other positions during the backswing that your weight does not shift to the back foot at any time. Keep your weight on the front foot even at the top of the backswing. (This is only for the pitch shot—not for full shots.)

It is important that the pace of the swing be consistent throughout. The pace is controlled by starting the downswing with a rotation of the torso and not with your arms. Any attempt to speed up through the hitting area will definitely cause inconsistent results. It is no good swinging slowly through one shot and quickly through the next. Try to imagine a pendulum and the way it moves backward and forward at the same pace. Try to follow this pace in all of your pitch shots.

The left arm stays straight throughout this entire shot from the address position (1), your backswing (2&3), impact position, and follow-through (4&5). A bent left arm will result in inconsistent direction and you'll also have a tendency to hit the ball thin (or blade the ball). Lastly, as you see here, it is important to follow-through. Do not stop your follow-through on this shot or you will constantly come up short. The follow-through should finish at about 3 o'clock (4&5).

And finally, be sure to follow-through directly at the target and not around your body. The hands should finish in about the middle of your chest (5).

With just a little practice to establish your distances and pace, you will find playing these shots a lot more fun. You'll also get a lot of comments from your playing partners such as "Where did you learn to pitch all of a sudden?"

1.

2.

3.

4.

5.

THE LOB SHOT

The difference between the pitch shot and a lob shot is that the lob shot is a much shorter, softer landing shot and will usually be played inside of 30 yards. Vital to the lob shot is the right equipment. You need a 60 degree wedge or a sand wedge with very little bounce.

To play this shot correctly you have to open the clubface and if you use a sand wedge with a high degree of "bounce" as in picture 1 the flange will strike the ground first causing the leading edge to hit the ball and a sculled shot will result.

In picture 2 you can see that with a 60 degree wedge you can open the clubface and still slide the clubhead under the ball.

TECHNIQUE

Take a fairly long backswing while fully cocking the wrists (1). Control the downswing with the torso and not the arms, maintaining the wrist cock and keeping the blade open throughout the shot (2). Finally the follow-through will end with the clubface still facing the sky (3).

The real secret of this shot is to not allow the fingers to pass the pad of the right hand. This shot takes a lot of practice in order to master the technique needed for success on the course. However, the results will have a positive effect on your score and you'll feel great satisfaction in having mastered this beautiful shot.

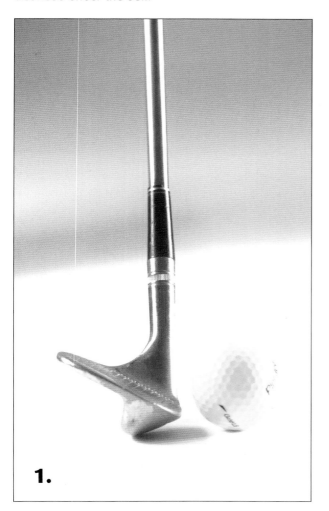

1.

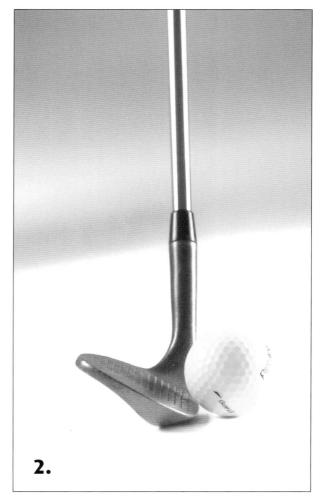

2.

WEDGE MANIA

There has been a lot of hype in the last few years over pitching, sand and lob wedges, but high handicap golfers do not have the skill to warrant more than three wedges, and the lower handicap golfer has enough skill to only need three wedges.

THE PITCHING WEDGE

Usually about 50 degrees in loft, this club is sometimes called a 10 iron, and should be used for full shots into the green (anywhere from 60 to 120 yards depending on your handicap) and chipping.

THE SAND WEDGE

Usually about 55 degrees, this club should not be restricted to the sand only. This very versatile club can be used from 50 to 110 yards with a full swing, sand play around the green, or chipping. Be careful on hardpan or fairly firm bunkers as the sand wedge has "bounce" as seen in the picture, causing the back edge of the flange to hit the ground first. This means that the leading-edge of the club would not get under the ball and you would scull the shot.

THE LOB WEDGE

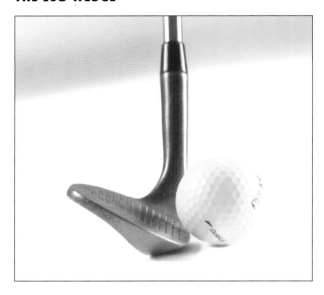

Usually about 60 degrees, this is the most versatile club in the bag and can be used for pitching, sand play (out of firm sand), and chipping. This club has very little or no bounce and can therefore get under the ball, even on hardpan or very tight lies on the fairway.

THE AUTHOR'S CLUBS

I carry a 50 degree pitching wedge, a 55 degree sand wedge, and a 60 degree lob wedge. This provides an equal gap between the three clubs, which gives me equal yardage not only with my full shots, but it allows me to control my distance pretty accurately with my pitch shots. This also eliminates the "gap" wedge sold with many sets, allowing me to carry an additional club for my longer shots.

AUTHOR'S SCALE OF PITCH SHOTS:
- 30 yards: 7 o'clock pitch shot—lob wedge
- 40 yards: 8 o'clock pitch shot—lob wedge
- 50 yards: 9 o'clock pitch shot—lob wedge
- 60 yards: 10 o'clock pitch shot—lob wedge
- 70 yards: 10 o'clock pitch shot—sand wedge
- 80 yards: 10 o'clock pitch shot—pitching wedge
- 90–95 yards: full swing—lob wedge
- 105–110 yards: full swing—sand wedge
- 120–125 yards: full swing—pitching wedge

Each golfer's yardages will be slightly different, so go out and practice these shots and make a "yardage chart" of your own.

Take any utility clubs, such as a gap wedge or any wedges that vary by only two or three degrees out of your bag and add some utility woods. Women and senior golfers particularly benefit more from carrying a 7 or 9 wood than having four wedges in their bag. There are some new utility clubs on the market called "middleclubs" which have a heavy head and a significantly shorter shaft than the usual utility clubs. Ask for advice from your local golf school on obtaining these clubs.

Make sure that the gaps in loft between your wedges are equal for increased accuracy and lower scores. Have the gaps measured at a reputable golf store, and have them bend the clubheads a few degrees up or down if they are not quite right.

Choose the right wedges for your game and with a little bit of practice with these clubs, you will take several shots off that handicap.

LEFT AND ABOVE LEFT: Middleclubs have a heavy head and are shorter than the usual utility clubs. Replacing 2 and 3 irons with the 2 and 3 middleclubs means you can hit the same distance, but with a club that is much easier to use.

CHIPPING

The golden rule in chipping is: fly the ball in the air as little as possible and roll the ball as much as possible. With that in mind, it is important to understand the airtime/ground-time ratios of shots hit with different clubs. The selection of the correct club is vital. You can chip with anything from a three iron to a sand wedge depending on the situation, but you must know the following formulas to decide which club is required.

THE 6-8-10 METHOD FOR CHIPPING

When you chip with a 10 iron (or pitching wedge as it is commonly called) the ball will fly half the distance to the hole and roll half the distance. When you chip with an 8 iron the ball will fly a third and roll for two thirds. When you chip with a 6 iron the ball will fly a quarter and roll for three-quarters.

These formulas are based on a normal paced, level green (a situation we don't often find on the course) so if you are chipping uphill you would need to go up one club and if you are chipping downhill you need to go down one club. If the green is fast, again you will need to go down one club and if the green is slow you will go up one club. This may sound confusing at first, but once you understand the basic formula, it really is just common sense from then on.

This table will help you understand the different clubs needed for various chipping situations. Remember, the landing spot is always about 3ft to 4ft onto the green.

CLUB	LEVEL	UPHILL / SLOW	DOWNHILL / FAST
6 iron	Fly ¼; roll ¾	5 iron	7 iron
8 Iron	Fly ⅓; roll ⅔	7 iron	9 iron
PW	Fly ½; roll ½	9 iron	sand wedge

THE TECHNIQUE

At the address position the weight is on the front foot, with the ball position in the middle of the feet. The hands are slightly ahead of the ball.

In order to land the ball on the correct spot, you need to make your practice swings looking at where you want to land the ball and not at the ground. By doing this your subconscious will determine how hard you need to hit the ball to fly it in the air the correct distance.

By doing a backward and forward motion continually, called the "brush brush shot," you will eventually develop the feel necessary to fly the ball any distance you want (1 to 4).

IMPORTANT ASPECTS OF CHIPPING

The most important aspect of chipping (besides choosing the right club) is to make sure that the left wrist (right wrist for left-handers) does not break down (or bend) during the chipping motion.

The moment the wrist breaks down two things start to happen:

1. The loft on the club changes, therefore changing the trajectory, which in turn affects the roll of the ball. Inconsistent distances will result.

2. The arm bends as well, causing bladed shots that go screaming across the green.

To ensure that neither of these things happens, work on keeping your arm straight and your wrist firm during the shot. If you find this difficult to achieve in practice try taking a thick rubber band and placing it around your wrist. Slide the butt end of the club under the elastic band, keeping the butt end of the club close to the wrist. This will give you the correct feel when chipping the ball.

If you wish to lower your handicap, miss a few sessions on the driving range, and head for the chipping green instead. You'll love the results to your game, but your opponents won't!

RIGHT: Work on keeping your arm straight and your wrist firm during a chipping shot.

OTHER CLUBS TO CHIP WITH

FAIRWAY WOODS

Do not limit yourself to chipping only with specific clubs but rather use the right club for the right situation. If you are in fluffy grass around the green try chipping with a 3 or 5 wood. The large soleplate will prevent the club from getting caught up in the grass and the loft will lift the ball over the fringe and get it rolling on the green fairly quickly. It is easy to have a high success rate with this shot without much practice (1 & 2).

THE BELLIED WEDGE

When the ball is sitting up against the fringe of the green it is sometimes difficult to get the putterface on the ball. Use your sand wedge and strike the ball on the equator (3), causing the ball to roll away from the fringe smoothly (4). You should hit this shot as hard as you would have done with your putter.

THE "TEXAS WEDGE"

The Texas wedge refers to the use of your putter from off the green. They say that in Texas it is so windy you have to keep the ball on the ground as much as possible. Use this shot when the fringe between you and the green is fairly smooth and the putting surface is fairly fast.

Anytime you feel that it would be difficult landing the ball on the green with a chip and stop the ball at the flag, consider the Texas wedge. Remember to hit the putt a little firmer to compensate for going through the fringe.

The general rule of thumb is for every foot of fringe you have to putt through, add a foot to the distance of the putt. For example, if you have a 20ft putt to make, and 4ft of that distance was through the fringe, hit the putt as hard as you would hit a putt for 24ft.

The sequence of photographs (1 to 14) show the Texas wedge in action.

PRACTICING YOUR CHIPPING AT HOME

Another aspect of your short game that you can work on indoors is chipping. One of the big keys to chipping is "feel." You can develop this while at home when you don't have time to go to the practice area.

Set up a spare piece of carpet (1). Place a small object (in this case a business card) out about 6ft away to mark a landing spot. Do the practice swing looking at the card to get the "feel" of how hard you need to hit the ball (2).

Chip the ball and attempt to land it on the card (3 & 4). If you can perfect this at home, you will be able to land the ball where you want to on the golf course.

If you can also understand the airtime/ground-time ratios of your clubs (see table on page 112), your chipping will definitely improve.

GOALS FOR CHIPPING TECHNIQUE

Work on your technique to:

1. Perfect the execution of the chipping stroke.
2. Develop "feel" in order to hit the ball in the air the required distance.

PUTTING

The single most important aspect of putting is alignment and most golfers aim incorrectly. The main reason for this is that our eyes are not designed to aim from a sideways position. All other sports that require aiming are face-on and therefore our eyes are focusing in a natural way. When we put our putter behind the ball, we get an optical illusion as to where we are aiming. This alignment can be as much as 4in off from 10ft.

The only way to line up correctly is to first put a stripe on your ball. A small plastic device designed for this purpose is available in most golf stores. Take the ball and draw a line halfway around the equator, making sure not to cover up the printing. Once you have established the correct line along which to putt, place the ball on the ground with the line on the ball along this target line.

Place your putter behind the ball making sure that the line on the putter and the line on the ball are all on the same straight line. Now that you are aligned correctly, go ahead and putt the ball. If the stroke is good, you should see the line on the ball rolling end over end. If this is not happening, place a board along the outside of your putter to help you keep the putterhead moving in a straight line toward the target.

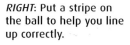

RIGHT: Put a stripe on the ball to help you line up correctly.

THE PUSH DRILL

The first drill is designed to help you kinesthetically feel the correct movement of the arms and hands throughout the putting stroke. The overall objective is to allow absolutely no breakdown between the forearm of the leading arm and the putter shaft. This ensures a perfect pendulum stroke. It also helps tremendously with distance control because the hands are completely passive and will not get involved in "hitting" the ball, which causes loss of distance control. This drill takes six weeks to perfect, but you can practice at any time, at the office or at home for just a few minutes a day.

WEEK 1

You need a straight edge of some kind in order to do this drill, such as a yardstick. Put the putter directly behind the ball (1). Without taking the clubhead back, simply push the putterhead through, keeping the toe of the putter along the yardstick. The putterface stays at 90 degrees to the yardstick and the putterhead is low to the ground (2).

You do not need a target to aim at, just make sure you feel the upper part of the leading arm controlling this movement and not the hands. The angle between the leading arm and the shaft should not change.

WEEK 2

Place the ball in the middle of the yardstick and place the putter 6in behind the ball. Now push the putterhead through to 12in beyond where the ball was, again making sure that you feel the upper part of the leading arm controlling the "push" with no breakdown between the forearm and the shaft. The toe of the putter must stay parallel to the ruler, and the putterface must remain square.

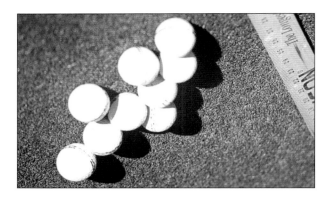

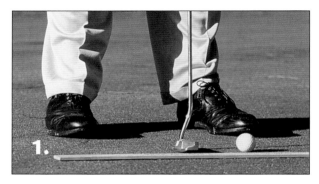

WEEK 3

Finally, put all of this together by making a continuous putting stroke, still using the ruler and still taking the putterhead back half the distance of the follow-through. Pay attention to detail and ensure that the toe of the putter stays on the yardstick and the putterface remains square 100 percent of the time. You won't derive any benefit from these drills if you do not pay attention to what the putterhead is doing. Remember, in weeks 1, 2 and 3 there is no target, allowing you to focus strictly on the putting motion.

WEEK 4

Go back to the same drill as week 1, but now use a target (3). If you're on a putting green use the hole; if you are at home use a putting cup.

WEEK 5

Do the same drill as week 2, but also with a target. The target needs to be a little further away than it was in week 4.

WEEK 6

Finally, do the same drill as in week 3 but with a target. The target needs to be a little further away than in week 5.

The reason you do not have a target for the first three weeks is to make you focus on what the putterhead is doing and not what the ball is doing. If you had a target your attention would be on seeing the ball go into the hole and the true focus of watching the putterhead would be lost.

3.

FREQUENTLY ASKED QUESTIONS

"Doesn't the push drill make you start to 'push' your putts?"
It is important while doing the push drill that you use a ruler or something that will help you push the putter "straight" through. The toe of the putter must stay an equal distance from the ruler at all times. This way the putterhead is always on line. And the face of the putter must at all times be at 90 degrees to the ruler in order for the ball to roll on the exact line you want.

"How does this drill work when putting normally?"
A drill is to be used only on the practice green so you can train yourself to repeat it competently over and over. Later when you are on the course you don't have to think of the drill—you will automatically have a good putting stroke. Once you have chosen the line you can keep focused only on the speed needed to hit the putt, something all great putters do.

"I thought you weren't supposed to be right hand dominant when you putted?"
The push drill is to help you feel the arm and hands "kinesthetically" through the putting stroke and the objective is not to feel breakdown between the arms and hands. This means that there is no "dominant hand or arm" when you putt. By doing the push drill you will finally feel the big muscles in the shoulders and upper back controlling the putting motion, eliminating the small muscles of the arms and hands which are the real "killers" in the putting stroke.

Remember that each of the push drills needs to be practiced (either at home or on the putting green) for at least one week in order to develop a completely automatic motion.

REPETITIVE PUTT DRILL

Short putts, those between 4 and 6ft, are the ones we expect to make most of the time. Research shows, however, that the touring pros make only about 50 percent of 6ft putts, so the average golfer should not get too frustrated when their percentage is lower. However, with intelligent practice, you can do something to increase that percentage.

HOW TO PRACTICE

Take ten balls and line up a straight putt of about 3 to 4ft using a straight edge to help ensure that the putter is moving straight back and through. You could also use a teaching aid (shown below), which helps you keep the putterhead straight.

It is important to practice a straight putt, because then you need only focus on the stroke and not on the break. Obviously if you miss a straight putt you will know that you made a bad stroke. If you miss a breaking putt, you may have made a good stroke

BELOW: This teaching aid helps to ensure that the putter moves straight back and through.

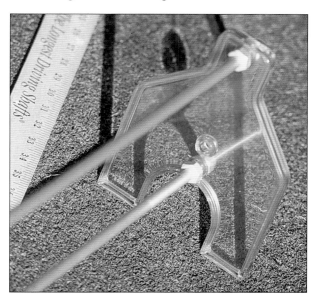

but just had the wrong speed. As we are working on the stroke here and not "feel," pick a straight putt.

Now, start putting with two objectives:

1   Make sure the putterhead is going straight back as in picture 1, and straight through as in 2.

2   Make sure the putterface is square to your line at all times (also noted in picture 2). This is the most common fault with poor putters and requires much work and concentration, but will have huge benefits if you have the determination to get it right.

Set yourself a goal for the number of putts that you can hole in a row. Gradually increase this goal until you can get up to 50. Remember; if you miss one you have to start at number one again.

This teaches you how to putt under pressure, because as you reach 45, 46, 47, 48, you don't want to start at one again so you must make a good stroke.

The secondary benefit of this practice method is to your subconscious. As you hole putt after putt at this distance, your confidence escalates and you have less and less fear of these putts. If you don't have time to go to the course, you can practice this at home on the carpet. This is a great way to get your putting stroke solid for next spring, especially for those of you who are stuck indoors for the winter.

DEVELOP THE "FEEL" OF A PRO

Usually, when we three-putt, it's because we have left the first putt either too long or too short. Rarely do we leave our first putt too wide left or right of the hole. The reason for this is what is known as "lack of feel" for the shot.

What is this thing called "feel?" Is it something that exists in our hands? No, feel exists in your subconscious. Take a ball and throw it to a target; not only do you not think of your target distance in feet and inches, you don't consider how far back to take your hand to achieve this distance. This is because we grew up as kids throwing a ball and our subconscious knows exactly how hard to throw the ball to reach the target. So if you want to develop good feel as a golfer, you have to train your subconscious to know exactly how hard to hit your long putts.

THE METHOD

Set up about 20 balls and aim for a target approximately 35ft away (1). Once you have lined up, putt the ball at the target looking at the hole and not at the ball (2).

Now this may feel a little weird at first, but you'll soon get used to it. Remember, do not look at the ball when you putt, look at the hole. If you hit your first putt too soft (2), then hit your next putt a little harder (3), still looking at the hole. If you hit that putt too soft, then hit the next one a little harder (4). Continue this with each ball until you get the feel for exactly how hard to hit the putt (5).

Once you have hit all the balls to your target (6), pick a new target and start all over again. Remember, though, this is a practice drill for the putting green only. When you are on the course, take your practice swings looking at the target, but once you're lined up, look at the ball to ensure solid contact with the center of the putterface.

PUTTING POSTURE

There is no specific putting posture. If you follow the drills described here and the putterhead is traveling towards the target with the putterface square to your intended line, it matters less how you stand. However, here are a few postures that have worked well over the years for some great golfers.

Jack Nicklaus liked to "crouch" over his putts and used more of a "piston" action with his right forearm to move the putter straight through (1).

Raymond Floyd liked to stand more upright, and in fact used a slightly longer putter to allow himself to do this (2). He felt this posture allowed him to see the line a lot better.

1.

2.

3.

BALL POSITION

Play the ball about 2in inside your left heel (3), but move the ball forward if you have a severe downhill putt (4). This allows you to hit the ball with a little loft, giving a softer hit. Move the ball back in your stance for a severe uphill putt (5), which delofts the putter, imparting a little topspin on the ball and allowing you to get the ball up the slope without having to hit the ball quite as hard as you would from a normal position.

4.

5.

HAZARDS AND TROUBLE SHOTS

When you have a normal lie in a bunker and the pin is in the middle of the green, you want to play the greenside bunker as a standard bunker shot.

GREENSIDE BUNKER SHOT

Using your sand wedge, set up with your feet slightly open to the target, the clubface slightly open, and your weight set mostly on your front foot (1). Aiming about 2in behind the ball, swing the clubhead back and through along the intended line, making sure to finish the swing (see 2 to 9 following pages).

Two of the most critical components of this shot are: first, to make sure that your left arm does not break down; and second, to control the shot with your body rotation, and not with your arms. The most common mistake golfers make in the bunker is to try and "scoop" the ball out, resulting in the left arm breaking down and the weight moving towards the back foot. This produces either a sculled shot or the club enters the sand too far behind the ball, causing the clubhead to decelerate and the ball to remain in the bunker.

The bunker shot is just another pitch shot, so control your distance in the same way as you would a pitch shot. However, as you are hitting 2in behind the ball, the ball will obviously not go as far as with a pitch shot. The general rule of thumb is that the ball goes about half the distance. So if your 9 o'clock pitch shot went 50 yards, your 9 o'clock bunker shot will go about 25 yards.

1.

2.

3.

4.

5.

6.

7.

8.

When you first start working on bunker shots, draw a line in the sand about 2in behind the ball, and practice hitting that line consistently. This is an absolute must if you want to become a good bunker player. If you are hitting too far behind the ball, chances are you are starting your downswing with your arms and not with body rotation. Starting the downswing with the arms is an absolute no-no. If you have rotated your body correctly, you will finish the swing with all your weight on your front foot, your arms extended out in front of you and your belt buckle facing the target (9). Work towards this end, and you will become a consistent player out of the sand. The sequence (1 to 8) on the following pages shows the greenside bunker shot in profile.

9.

1.

2.

3.

4.

FAIRWAY BUNKERS

Fairway bunkers are installed by architects for one of two reasons. They either want to make the hole more difficult or they want to add an aesthetic value to the hole. In either case fairway bunkers are best avoided. However, we have all been in a fairway bunker at one time or another so it is important to understand how to play from these hazards.

The bunkers in North America are generally fairly shallow and allow golfers to advance the ball either well down the fairway or on to the green. In countries such as Scotland and Ireland, fairway bunkers are much deeper and present more of a penalty if you venture into one. It sometimes requires a sideways shot to extricate oneself from the hazard.

Once you are in the bunker, you have to decide which club you are going to use. Obviously the distance to your target is a deciding factor; the other factor is the height of the front lip of the bunker. In order to decide the choice of club, stand outside the bunker, lay your club flat on the ground and stand on the clubface. The resulting shaft angle will give you an approximate trajectory of the ball with that particular club. You can then decide whether that club will get the ball safely over the lip of the bunker. It is far better to take a more lofted club and come up a little short of your target than to use a less lofted club and end up burying the ball in the face of the bunker.

With your chosen club, take your normal stance and play the ball very slightly further back in your stance (right). Do not dig your feet into the sand as you would in a greenside bunker, as this will put your feet slightly lower than the ball causing a tendency to hit behind the ball and you will come up short of your target.

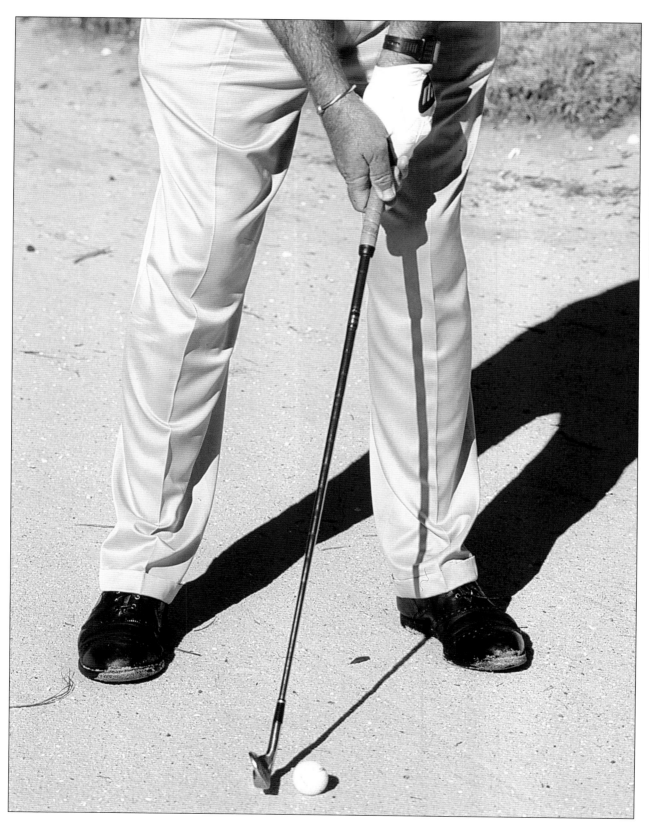

Try to make as smooth a swing (1&2) as possible so that your feet do not slip, and finish with a full follow-through with all your weight on your front foot (3).

Any attempt to "scoop" the ball in order to get it up will cause the clubhead to enter the sand behind the ball and a "fat" shot will result.

1.

2.

3.

PLAYING TO A CLOSE FLAGSTICK

When the flagstick is really close and you need to stop the ball in a hurry, a slightly different technique is necessary. The best thing to use is a 60 degree lob wedge for this shot (see below). Open the clubface and position yourself in a slightly open stance (1). Take the clubhead outside the target line on the back-swing (2, 3 & 4 overleaf) and hit only 1in behind the ball with a slight cutting motion (5, 6 & 7 overleaf). This will give the ball both height and spin and will allow it to stop very quickly (8, 9 & 10 overleaf). This is a shot that requires a lot of practice as hitting only 1in behind the ball allows for only a very small margin of error.

1.

2.

3.

4.

5.

7.

8.

9.

6.

10.

BALL NEAR FACE OF BUNKER

This is a shot that often intimidates people but again, the correct technique will always get the ball out. Open the clubface, make a bigger swing than normal, and make sure to follow-through. Do not let the bank in front of your ball make you stop your follow-through. Again, a little practice to develop confidence in the shot and the understanding that it must be played aggressively will lead to better shots in this situation in the future.

LONG PITCH FROM BUNKER

This is one of the most difficult shots in golf as there is no margin for error. It is played exactly the same as a normal pitch shot with one exception. The ball position is played slightly back of center in order to allow the hands to pass the ball early in the downswing (1). This enables the clubhead to hit the ball with a fairly steep descending blow. Follow-through in the normal manner (2). Control distance with your 7, 8, or 9 o'clock backswing. The ball trajectory will be a little lower but with plenty of backspin so the ball should still go the same distance as a regular pitch shot. Do not attempt to pick this shot clean off the sand as you will have a tendency to hit slightly behind the ball leaving it short of your target and sometimes still in the sand. Pictures 3 to 6 below show the pitch shot in profile.

BURIED LIE IN BUNKER

The buried lie in a bunker is an easier shot than most people think. Instead of opening the clubface, this time you must close it so that the clubface is aiming towards your front toe (above). The secret to this shot is to make sure that your grip pressure is very loose. Still hit 2in behind the ball, and as the toe of the club enters the sand, it digs in because of the closed clubface. However, because of the loose grip the force of the sand will twist the club slightly in your hands squaring the clubface off and popping the ball out of the sand. This ball will land with a lot of topspin so plan to land this ball well short of the hole.

3.

BALL IN BACK OF BUNKER

When the ball is in the back of the bunker, usually the back edge hinders the takeaway and downswing. By using a "tomahawk shot" you can extricate the ball fairly easily. Address the ball with one foot outside the bunker (1) and start the takeaway almost vertically (2, 3 & 4). This will eliminate the back edge of the bunker. Bring the club back down to the ball on this vertical plane and let the club enter the sand about 2in behind the ball (5, 6 & 7). At this moment "chicken wing" your left arm, pulling the clubhead across the ball. The result is a fairly high soft shot coming out of the bunker with quite a bit of left to right spin, so aim well left of the hole (8, 9 & 10).

1.

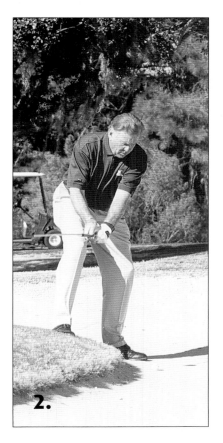

2.

3.

4.

1.

2.

HITTING OFF HARDPAN

Treat hardpan in the same way as a regular fairway shot with one exception. If you are playing an iron shot the normal ball position on the fairway is 2in inside your left heel (1 & 2). Off hardpan the ball position is directly off your left heel, allowing you to catch the ball right at the bottom of the arc almost like a fairway wood. This allows you to "clip" the ball off hardpan without hitting a divot. If you hit down too steeply on hardpan the club might "jar" and you could injure yourself.

DRAWS AND FADES

When faced with an obstacle such as the tree in front, your option is to go under, over, left, or right of the tree. As the green is 250 yards away, under is not an option, and neither is over as you could not get your shot with the 3 wood up in the air fast enough. Your choices are to either fade the ball down the left side or draw the ball down the right side. If you aim to the right over the hazard and the ball does not draw, the ball will end up in the hazard. If you aim to the left and the ball does not fade, the ball will end up out of bounds, which is even worse. The correct shot to play is the one you feel most confident in.

HITTING AN INTENTIONAL DRAW

First aim your feet, hips, and shoulders slightly to the right of your target (1). Start your backswing by taking the club back a little more inside the target line than normal, causing you to have a slightly flatter backswing (2). Start the downswing by dropping your hands straight down and keeping them very close to the body. Make sure you exaggerate the inside-out action of the clubhead, at the same time allowing your hands to roll over through the hitting area.

1.

2.

Stay down on this shot (3), as an early straightening of the spine will prevent the correct release and the ball will be left out to the right. If you have confidence in your ability to draw the ball, be totally committed to the shot. You will be rewarded with a nice, high draw.

HITTING AN INTENTIONAL FADE

Start out by aiming your feet, hips, and shoulders to the left of target (1). Start the backswing by taking the clubhead slightly outside the target line, creating a fairly steep backswing (2).

Start the downswing with an early clearing of the left side which will cause an outside-in clubhead path. Hold off releasing the hands for as long as possible which will create a nice high fade (3 & 4). As with the draw shot, be totally committed and trust your swing to create the shot.

PLAYING LEFT-HANDED SHOTS

For right-handed players this is a really great shot to have in your arsenal when you find yourself against a tree where a left-handed shot is required. With a little practice, you will be able to advance the ball a reasonable distance instead of taking a penalty drop. Choose a club like a pitching wedge or 9 Iron because they have a larger face, flip the club over so that the toe is pointing to the ground, and address the ball in a left handed manner (1). Keep the backswing short, making sure that you keep the right arm straight throughout the shot (2). This creates a perfect arc which will ensure that the club face gets back to the ball squarely (3).

This shot needs to be practiced on the driving range before you ever try it on the golf course. However, the work is worth it as it has saved me many strokes over the years.

1.

2.

3.

PLAYING OUT OF HEAVY ROUGH

When playing out of heavy rough, your first objective should be to get the ball back into play. Advance the ball to an area that will make the next shot an easy one to the green. Depending on the height of the rough, choose a club with enough loft to get the ball airborne easily. With this particular shot you want to use a fairly tight grip, particularly with the last three fingers of the left hand (1). Out of heavy rough the clubface will have a tendency to shut down as the grass wraps around the hosel, so a firm grip will help prevent this. On the back-swing you want to have a fairly quick wrist cock so that the grass does not catch the clubhead (2, 3 & 4). You also want to produce a fairly steep downswing so that the clubhead gets to the ball as quickly as possible (5). Make sure you keep the club moving through the grass by maintaining a good body rotation through the impact area to a full follow-through (6 & 7).

1.

2.

3.

PLAYING OUT OF WATER

If the ball is not completely submerged but is lying just under the surface of water then a shot can be played. Play it just like a bunker shot, aiming about 2in behind the ball and swinging about twice as hard as a regular bunker shot (1 to 8). A towel tucked in at the belt, covering your pants or skirt, will prevent water and mud from soiling your clothing. This shot must be played aggressively and as with any bunker shot a full follow-through is critical (9 to 11 overleaf).

1.

2.

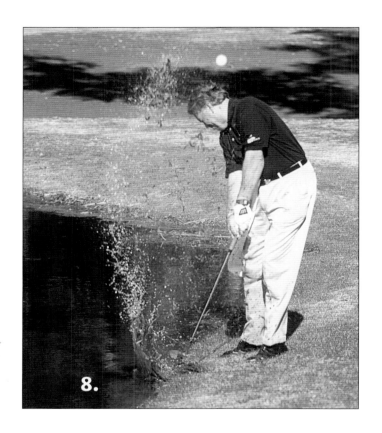

8.

9.

10.

11.

1.

UPHILL AND DOWNHILL LIES

Most students, including low handicap players, are confused as how to play the ball from uphill and downhill lies. This uncertainty often results in bad shots. So let's set out a few principles.

UPHILL LIES

The ball position needs to be forward in the stance and your body tilted almost perpendicular to the slope (1). Most of your weight should be on your back foot (2) as you make the shot.

After completing the shot, your weight should still be on your back foot (3). This is one of the few shots in golf where there is no weight shift. If you try to shift your weight to the front foot you will raise your body and top the ball.

A FEW TIPS TO REMEMBER:

1. Take at least one extra club (a 7 iron instead of an 8), or maybe two if the slope is a severe one.
2. Aim to the right (for right-handed golfers) as the tendency is to pull the ball.
3. On uphill or downhill lies, always play the ball off your highest foot (in this case the front foot).

2.

3.

DOWNHILL LIES

The ball should be positioned back in your stance and your body tilted almost perpendicular to the slope (1). Most of your weight should be on your front foot.

If the ball was positioned incorrectly towards the front foot you would tend to hit behind the ball as the ground behind the ball is higher than the ball.

The follow-through is shortened (3). If you to follow-through all the way the momentum would pull you off balance.

A FEW TIPS TO REMEMBER:

1. Take one club less (an 8 instead of a 7) and play the ball off the back foot which decreases the loft and increases distance.

2. Aim to the left (for right-handed golfers) as the ball will tend to fade.

3. On uphill or downhill lies always play the ball off your highest foot (in this case the back foot).

BALL BELOW THE FEET

A ball below your feet on a sidehill lie is the most difficult of all sloping lies. Do not bend your knees too much in order to reach the ball. This will tend to make you rise up as you swing through causing you to top the ball. Keep your legs at their normal flex and bend over more from the waist (1). As long as you maintain your spine angle, you will not rise up (2 & 3).

A FEW TIPS TO REMEMBER:

1. Sustain your normal knee flex and bend a little more from the waist.
2. Keep the backswing short (2). If you try to swing to your normal position there will be a tendency to rise up.
3. Take one more club (an 8 instead of a 9) .
4. Aim to the left as the ball will have a tendency to fade or go to the right (for right-handed golfers).

BALL ABOVE THE FEET

When the ball is above your feet, in order to keep your normal posture you must grip the club a little shorter (1). If you do not, the club will hit the ground first. Straightening the body and especially the legs, to compensate for the club feeling too long, will tend to make you lose your balance very easily—something you do not want at any time.

A FEW TIPS TO REMEMBER:

1. Take one club more (a 7 instead of an 8) and play the ball off the middle of your stance.

2. Aim to the right (for right-handed golfers) as the ball will tend to hook or pull.

3. Grip the club shorter (1). The amount of slope will determine how much shorter to grip, a greater slope means a shorter grip to make sure you are in your normal posture.

4. Make as smooth a swing as possible (2 & 3). Don't try and pull the ball back on line as it will do that on its own.

1.

2.

3.

STEEP SLOPES

When you find yourself on a steep bank around the green, stance can be a major problem as the slope will tend to throw you backwards making you lose your balance. Or, if your weight is on your back foot when you play the shot you'll sometimes tend to scuff behind ball. Place your back foot at 90 degrees to the shot, either in the bunker on the slope, and place your front foot perpendicular to the slope (1). This lets your left knee move out of the way and allows you to lean your body forward putting a weight on the ball of your front foot. Your hands stay ahead of the clubhead allowing you to make clean contact with the ball and maintain your balance throughout the shot (2 to 6 overleaf).

4.

5.

6.

HIGH SHOTS

CLUB SELECTION

To hit the ball high over an obstacle such as a tree or bush you must first select a club with enough loft to get you over the obstacle. A good way to do this is to lay the club you have selected down on the ground and stand on the clubface. The shaft angle produced will give you an approximate trajectory of that particular club. Give yourself a reasonable margin of error.

BALL POSITION

The ball should be 2 to 3in further forward than usual at the address position (1).

WEIGHT DISTRIBUTION

Your weight should be slightly towards your back foot, with your back shoulder lower than normal and your hands very slightly behind the clubhead. Stand behind the ball and visualize the trajectory going easily over the tree or bush and landing safely at your target.

THE SHOT

Take a normal backswing, and on the follow-through keep the club low through the hitting area and finish with a nice high follow-through (2). This swing should produce a higher than normal trajectory.

LOW SHOTS

CLUB SELECTION

You need to select a club with very little loft, perhaps a 4 or 5 iron. (Do not select a 2 or 3 iron, because the ball position is back and there is not enough loft on these clubs to get the ball airborne and a smothered shot will result.)

BALL POSITION

The ball needs to be back in the stance with the hands well ahead of the clubhead (1).

FOLLOW-THROUGH

The follow-through must be short and straight through to the target (6 &7). (A long, full follow-through will result in a higher trajectory.)

KEY FACTORS

Set the weight forward while executing the shot. Make sure that the left arm stays absolutely straight through impact (2 to 5). The slightest breakdown of the left arm will cause the clubhead to overtake the hands, and the ball will immediately go higher and crash into those overhanging branches.

This shot takes a little practice, so next time you're on the range, experiment with different clubs, and see just how low and far you can hit the ball. It will pay dividends on the course.

FAULTS AND PROBLEM-SOLVING

S ome of the most common faults in golf can be easily solved, once the golfer has analyzed their problem and made the appropriate changes. Outlined in this section are some of the faults often faced by many golfers with their solutions.

SLICING

When the ball curves significantly from left to right (for right-handed golfers) slicing occurs. Slicing is caused by the clubhead path cutting across the ball from the outside in. The clubface angle is open at impact, imparting spin on the ball and causing it to veer offline. As there are several swing flaws that can cause a slice, each one will be addressed separately:

FAULT: Starting the backswing with the clubhead moving outside the target line.
The hands have moved away from the body line causing the clubhead to move outside the target line on the backswing (1).
Halfway down the downswing the hands are too far away from the body and the clubhead is outside the hands ensuring an outside-in clubhead path (2).

1.

2.

The resulting downswing will cause the clubhead to finish low across the body producing a slice (3).
From the front angle notice that the hands have finished below shoulder level (4). This is a sure sign of a pull or a slice.

3.

4.

In summary, when you start the clubhead outside the target line, it causes the backswing to become too steep, which then causes the hands to move away from the body on the downswing. The clubhead gets outside the hands on the downswing and finally the clubhead cuts across the ball with the follow-through finishing low across the body.

CURE: Start the backswing keeping the clubhead slightly outside the hands (5).

5.

6.

Halfway up the backswing, make sure the shaft is pointing either at the ball or slightly inside (6).

The downswing is started with a lateral slide of the hips keeping the clubhead behind the hands as long as possible (7).

7.

The hands must travel down the body line in order for the clubhead path to stay on line.

8.

Make sure the hands move straight back along the body line and complete the backswing with your torso (and not your arms) which will allow the club to swing back on plane (8). (The backswing plane is a line drawn from the ball through the shoulders). The downswing is started with a lateral slide of the hips ensuring that the clubhead stays behind the hands on the way down. This will produce an inside-out clubhead path on a line that allows the club to travel more towards the target producing a straighter shot.

FAULT: The right elbow has drifted away from the body causing the backswing to become too steep (9).

CURE: At the top of the backswing the right arm should be in a "tray" position (10).

Allowing the right elbow to drift away from the body on the backswing causes the right forearm to get into a horizontal position at the top of the backswing. This causes the downswing to become too steep which in turn causes the clubhead to cut across the ball and produce a slice.

Make sure the right arm folds on the backswing keeping the elbows the same distance apart as they were at address. The forearm finishes at the top of the swing more perpendicular to the ground like a waiter carrying a tray. This allows the arms to drop down keeping the clubhead behind the hands and producing an inside-out path.

Work on taking the club back correctly, making sure the right forearm is in the correct position and the left arm is on plane. Start the downswing with a lateral slide of the hips which will allow the club to drop down keeping the clubhead behind the hands. Finally, make sure the clubhead stays on line to the target for as long as possible through impact and allow the hands to release through the shot in order to square the clubface.

PULLING

When the ball flies left of your target line, this is known as pulling.

FAULT: Pulling happens when the clubhead path is moving from the outside in, but the clubface angle is square to the path. The ball travels in a straight line, but misses the target to left. This is caused by one of two things.

The downswing is started with the upper body causing the clubhead to move outside the hands on the downswing, resulting in an outside-in clubhead path (1). Or, the left hip rotates too soon as the downswing is started, again causing the clubhead to move outside the hands.

As the hands move through the impact position, they rotate squaring the clubface angle to the clubhead path, and a straight pull will be the result (2).

1.

2.

CURE: Start the downswing with a lateral slide of the hips allowing the hands to drop down close to the bod (3). The clubhead stays behind the hands, the clubhead path moves more from the inside, and the arms travel down the body line (4).

3.

4.

1.

2.

HOOKING

When the ball curves strongly from right to left (for right-handed golfers), it is known as hooking. There are two types of hooking faults, the push hook and the pull hook.

PUSH HOOK

FAULT: The push hook is a shot that starts out to the right and moves back to the target, and a pull hook starts left and curves even further to the left.

The push hook results from the clubhead traveling too severely from the inside to out and the hands rotating too quickly. This is caused by the backswing starting out too flat (1) and the club shaft being laid off on the backswing (2).

This enables the clubhead to get too far on the inside on the downswing forcing the club to strike the ball in a severe inside-out motion. Combined with the wrist rotation (3), the ball moves out to the right of the target and then hooks back severely.

3.

CURE: Make sure to swing the club back on the correct plane (4) so that on the downswing the clubhead is slightly behind the hands (5), which allows the clubhead to travel more directly down the line toward the target (6). This position might produce a slight draw, which is desirable. Stay in the correct posture throughout the sequence and don't let your eyes follow the ball until it is well on its way to the hole.

5.

4.

6.

THE PULL HOOK

Like the slice, the pull hook, sometimes called a duck hook, is a totally undesirable shot. The ball starts off left of the target and hooks even further left, usually landing in trouble.

FAULT: The pull hook is usually caused by a spin-out of the left hip causing the shoulders to over-rotate and the arms to be thrown away from the body (1 & 2). The clubhead path comes from outside-in. If the hands rotate through impact the combination of clubhead path and clubface angle will cause the ball to start left and hook even further left. There is a saying in golf, "You can talk to a slice, but a hook won't listen."

CURE: Make sure the downswing is started with the hips and not with the arms (3). If the left hip initiates the downswing and moves laterally towards the target for the first few inches, the hands will drop down close to the body keeping the clubhead slightly behind the hands, which allows the clubhead path to work more down the target line (4). This is a sure-fire way to prevent a pull hook.

PUSHING

The pushed shot is one that starts off straight right of the target without any curve.

FAULT: The push shot is the closest to being a good swing without the ball hitting the target. Most elements of the golf swing are correct during a push shot with one exception—the hands fail to release, leaving the clubface slightly open (1). Even though the clubhead path has the desired inside-out motion, the ball will travel to the right. In this shot (1), the clubface is still facing towards the sky instead of the toe pointing up, indicating a lack of rotation of the left forearm.

CURE: Make sure the hands release through the hitting area and that halfway through the follow-through the toe of the club is pointing towards the sky (2). This ensures a square clubface position at impact.

1.

2.

TOPPING

Topping is caused by either a change of spine angle or collapsing the left arm through impact. In both instances the bottom of the arc will be above the ball and a topped shot will result.

FAULT: Topping is striking the middle or top half of the ball with the leading edge of the club causing the ball to bounce along the ground without any airtime at all (1&2). Almost all beginners tend to top the ball because they lack understanding of the true principles of ball striking.

CURE: When you are in your address position you are X number of inches from the ball. This X is made up by the length of the shaft, the length of your left arm, and your spine angle at address.

Any change in either the length of the left arm or spine angle will cause a topped shot. To prevent this from happening, make sure that you keep your

1.

2.

3.

left arm straight throughout the swing and your spine angle in the same position as your address position (3&4) when you swing through the ball (5).

5.

4.

OVERSWINGING

Many golfers think that overswinging occurs when the club shaft reaches beyond parallel at the top of the backswing, but this is not necessarily the case. There is a specific top of the backswing position for each golfer and this will mainly depend on the golfer's level of flexibility. A golfer who is extremely flexible like John Daly, who gets the club well beyond parallel at the top of the swing and still maintains a straight left arm and a restricted hip turn, is still well in control of the swing. On the other hand, someone like Doug Sanders, who had a short backswing, managed to hit the ball a long way and win many tournaments.

1.

2.

FAULT: Overswinging happens when the left arm collapses at the top of the backswing, or the hips over-rotate (1). This means a loss of that all important torque at the top of the backswing, which creates the speed on the downswing and follow-through.

CURE: Make sure the left arm is fully extended at the top of the backswing creating plenty of space between the right shoulder and hands (2). This also limits the amount of hip turn so that tightness is felt in the torso.

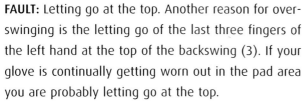

3.

4.

FAULT: Letting go at the top. Another reason for over-swinging is the letting go of the last three fingers of the left hand at the top of the backswing (3). If your glove is continually getting worn out in the pad area you are probably letting go at the top.

CURE: Keep the last three fingers of the left hand firmly on the club at the top of the backswing (4).

REVERSE PIVOT

The reverse pivot is another swing flaw that is created by overswinging, trying to take the club back too far in an attempt to hit the ball further.

In fact the opposite occurs as the weight tends to move to the back foot on the downswing, causing the golfer to hit behind the ball. Releasing the hands too early on the downswing means hitting the ball on the upswing with a resulting loss of power. A good turn is critical if distance is a problem in your golf swing.

FAULT: The spine angle tilts towards the target leaving the weight on the front foot (1 & 2). This usually causes the back leg to straighten which in turn causes the back hip to rise up making it difficult to start the downswing with a good weight shift as the weight is already on the front foot.

1.

2.

CURE: Get into your golf posture, leaning forward slightly from the waist and keeping your spine straight. Place a club along the inside of your back foot. This will act as a guide when you turn. Hold a club across your shoulders, making sure it is straight to get the correct alignment (3).

3.

Make a shoulder turn until the club across your shoulders is over the club inside your back heel and pointing in the same direction (4). You will feel that the weight has now moved on to the back foot with most of the weight towards the back heel. This position will give you a proper feel for where you need to be at the top of the backswing.

Now take the club that was across your shoulders and swing back until you feel you are in a similar position to where you were during the drill (5). From this backswing position you will have plenty of coil, which allows you to start your downswing with a good weight shift enabling you to hit the ball a lot further.

4.

5.

1.

2.

ERRORS IN THE ADDRESS POSITION

As I've mentioned earlier in this book the address position is vitally important to the start of a good golf swing. The correct address position includes a good posture, good knee flex, arms hanging comfortably from the body and hands placed in the correct position (1&2). Poor posture and address position can cause faults in your golf swing.

FAULT: Stance too narrow. A stance that is too narrow can cause poor balance on both the backswing and the follow-through (3).

CURE: Without the necessary balance you cannot produce good shots, so widen your stance a little.

3.

FAULT: A wide stance is adopted by golfers who try to hit the ball a long way (4). Their theory is that a wide stance will give them good stability and therefore they will be able to put a hard swing on the ball.

CURE: The opposite is true, as a wide swing restricts both the shoulder turn on the backswing and a good weight shift on the follow-through, which will hinder, not help distance. A narrower stance is advisable.

FAULT: Ball too far back in the stance. When the ball gets too far back in the stance (5) it creates a back-swing that is too steep, which results in the down-swing also being too steep. This causes you to hit down on the ball resulting in a low trajectory with iron shots and makes you "pop up" your tee shots.

CURE: Make sure the ball position is correct depending on the club you have in your hand.

4.

5.

FAULT: Hands too far behind ball. When the hands get too far behind ball (6) there is a tendency to start the backswing by cocking the wrists too early.

CURE: You want your arms, shoulders, and club to move in one motion as you start the backswing so it is important to have a straight line formed by your left arm and shaft all the way from the shoulder to the clubhead.

FAULT: Hands too far forward. When your hands are too far ahead of the ball it immediately puts your body out of position to make a good takeaway (7). The shoulders are forced into an "open" position and this address position usually causes the golfer to cut across the ball producing a slice.

CURE: Again, make sure that the left arm and shaft form a straight line from your shoulder to the ball.

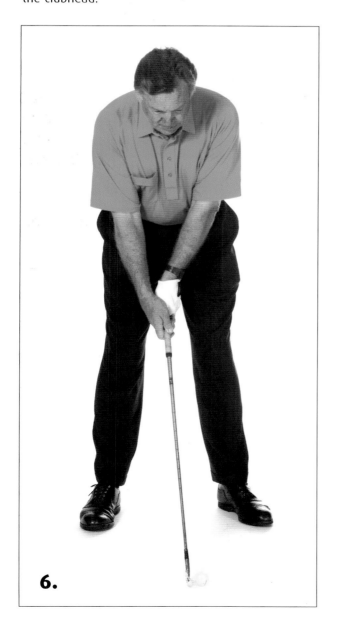

6.

7.

8.

FAULT: Standing too far from the ball.

When the golfer stands too far from ball it makes the spine bend too far over (8). This causes a change in spine angle on the backswing and the golfer raises his head in order to make a proper turn. On the downswing the golfer will attempt to get back down to the ball in order to make solid contact. However, this up and down motion leads to inconsistency in ball striking.

CURE: From your address position, take your right hand off the club, make a fist, and place the fist between the top of your left thigh and the butt of the club (9). This is a good guide to tell you how far your hands should be from your body in the address position.

FAULT: Standing too close to the ball.

When a golfer stands too close to the ball (10), there is a tendency to take the club away on a steep plane, causing them to cut across the ball on the downswing, producing a pull or a slice depending where the hands are at impact.

CURE: Again, use the "fist rule" (9) to gauge the correct distance from the ball in the address position.

9.

10.

GAINING POWER: KEEPING ACCURACY

Many golfers who attempt to add distance to their drives suddenly find that they have lost the accuracy they once had. Can you retain accuracy if you try to add power? The answer is definitely yes.

Often golfers believe they have to increase the length of the backswing in order to add power. This creates additional problems which can end up costing them distance instead of adding yardage.

2.

1.

3.

FAULT: The two most common errors are holding the right elbow too far away from the body (1), as the golfer thinks this makes a bigger turn and collapsing the left arm to get the clubhead past parallel at the top of the backswing (2), again thinking this helps them generate more clubhead speed. Both of these positions result in an "over the top" move, causing the club to travel across the target line and finish low across the body (3).

5.

4.

CURE: Make sure that the right arm stays in a position perpendicular to the ground at top of the backswing (4). The left arm must be fully extended to create tightness in the torso and this tightness or coil is called "torque" (5).

This position will help the right arm drop down into a good pre-impact position (6), ensuring that the clubhead travels down the target line through impact (7). Work on this move and you will gain more power while keeping your accuracy.

6.

7.

WEIGHT SHIFT

There is so much confusion regarding weight shift on the downswing that it needs explaining in detail. Weight shift is one of the key movements in the golf swing. It determines clubhead path and clubhead speed through impact. If you do not understand weight shift, you are going to lose both power and direction in your swing.

1.

2.

FAULT: Starting the weight shift with a rotation of the hips. When you start the downswing with a rotation of the hips instead of a lateral movement (1), the shoulders immediately follow the direction of the hips. This causes the shoulders to open too soon throwing the clubhead outside the hands which causes the clubhead path to cut across the ball, resulting in both power and direction loss (2).

FAULT: Starting the weight shift with a sway to the right.

3.

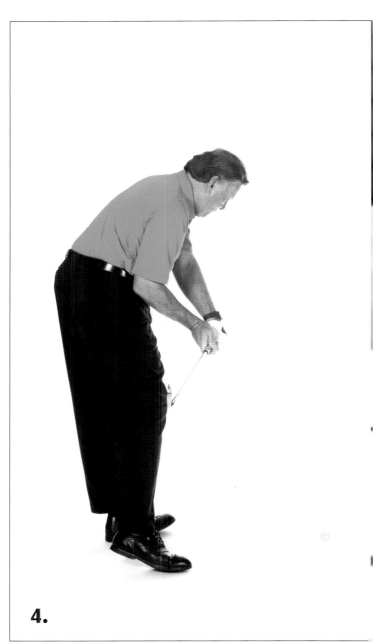

4.

Sometimes in an attempt to transfer the weight correctly, the golfer makes an exaggerated lateral slide of the hips (3). Although this does get the weight across to the front side, it causes the upper body to also move forward (4). Now the upper body is ahead of the ball at impact, leaving the clubface wide open causing loss of power and direction. Usually a huge slice or even a shank can occur from this motion.

FAULT: No weight shift at all

5.

6.

With no weight shift at all, the weight obviously stays on the back foot (5), causing the back shoulder to drop, the shoulders also open up, and the clubhead to cut across the ball (6). This is common with beginner golfers, and is a subconscious attempt to get the ball up into the air. There is very little power in this type of swing.

CURE: Shift the weight correctly.

7.

8.

Move the weight across from the back foot to the front foot with a "slight" lateral movement of the hips, making sure that they stay "square" until the weight is all onto the front foot and the back heel is slightly off the ground (7). If the heel is still flat, you have not transferred the weight correctly.

This automatically retains the angle between the left forearm and the shaft of the club (for right-handed golfers). The clubhead will release with maximum speed and you will keep the clubhead moving along the correct path through impact, producing a powerful and straight shot (8).

SHANKING

The shank is the most dreaded shot in golf. Once you start shanking it is almost like a virus, and it will penetrate the very depths of your psyche.

FAULT: The impact position of the ball is off the hosel of the club instead of the clubface, causing the ball to travel off line at 90 degrees to the intended target line of flight.

A shank is caused by one of two things: The hands move too far away from the body on the downswing (1), throwing the clubhead outside the hands and allowing the hosel to hit the ball first (2).

1.

2.

The other reason for shanking is starting the clubhead too much from the inside on the downswing, and not releasing the hands (3).

CURE: Address your ball after you have placed a second ball just outside of it (4).

The object is to miss the outside ball while hitting the inside ball. This forces you to keep the club on an inside path which will prevent you from shanking.

3.

4.

ERRORS IN PITCHING

There tends to be more errors in the short game than in the long game. When most amateurs go to the driving range to practice, they feel that they must work on their full swing to get their money's worth. Also, a lot of golfers find practicing their short game tedious and boring. And, of course, if you are not very good at the short game it can also be frustrating. Touring professionals spend over 50 percent of their practice time on the short game. Pros can chip, pitch, and get the ball out of sand close enough for one putt most of the time, but this does not happen by luck, only by extremely hard practice. As a friend Gary Player once said "The harder I practice, the luckier I get!" Short game guru Dave Peltz says that if an 18 handicap improved his or her short game from 50 yards in to the level of a scratch player, his handicap would plummet to 9. This should be great incentive for every high handicap golfer to work hard on their short game in order to reduce their handicap. You can work on chipping and putting at home, so for those who have hectic schedules, there is no excuse not to practice your short game for 15 or 20 minutes three times a week. As long as you are working with a purpose and understand your ultimate goals, these practice sessions should be fruitful.

FAULT: The infamous "chicken wing," or collapsing left arm.

Collapsing the left arm causes more bad shots in pitching than any other fault (1). As there is a tendency to try and lift the ball into the air instead of allowing the loft of the club to do the work, the left arm will inevitably "chicken wing" and a sculled shot will result. The left arm needs to be perfectly straight at the finish.

1.

2.

3.

CURE: Practice keeping your left arm straight through the hitting area and finish with both arms extended out in front of you (2 & 3). If your left arm is not straight at this point, extend it out until it is before you attempt the next shot. By working towards this finish position, you will ensure that your left arm stays straight throughout the shot.

FAULT: Changing the spine angle.

Golfers commonly refer to this as "lifting the head" (4). However, the problem actually occurs with the spine angle. As the head is attached to the spine it looks like the head is lifting. This straightening of the spine angle is again caused by a subconscious attempt to try and lift ball into the air. The golfer does not trust the loft of the club to do the work and in an attempt to give the ball higher flight they lift up their upper body and a sculled shot results.

CURE: Practice hitting pitch shots waiting for your right shoulder to get to your chin allowing your head to rotate or your body to straighten.

4.

FAULT: Starting the downswing with the arms.

5.

6.

CURE: Take your golf stance and practice tossing a ball underhand (6). To throw the ball any distance you have to turn your left hip out of the way and your hand holding the ball must travel towards the target (7). This is the same motion required for a good pitch shot.

If you have a tendency to hit your pitch shots heavy (behind the ball) then you are probably starting the downswing with your arms instead of allowing your torso to control this shot (5). From the top of the back-swing the first movement of the pitch shot is getting the left side out of the way fairly quickly keeping the body ahead of the arms and arms ahead of the club-head. This ensures that the hands will pass the ball before the clubhead gets there.

7.

Now take your club and practice attaining the same feeling. Hitting the ground behind the ball will become a thing of the past.

FAULT: Following through around the body.

8.

9.

Very often in an attempt to clear the left side, the follow-through ends up around the body causing the shot to be pulled to the left (8). Obviously the pitch shot is an accuracy shot, so it is no good getting the distance you want in the air, but being 10 or 15 yards offline to the left of your target.

CURE: Again, the underhand toss drill (6 & 7) is appropriate, giving you the feeling of your hands traveling directly through to the target. At the end of the swing, your hands should finish in front of your chest with the club shaft vertical (9).

FAULT: Scooping. This is another attempt by the golfer to help the ball up into the air. A scooping motion of the right hand forces the left wrist to "cup" keeping the clubface open and producing a sculled shot or a shot that flies fairly high coming up well short of the target (10).

11.

10.

CURE: Allow the right hand to cross over the left through the hitting area, keeping the back of the left wrist flat at all times (11). This rotation not only squares the clubface at impact, but produces the correct loft and distance control definitely improves.

ERRORS IN CHIPPING

FAULT: Breakdown of the wrist.

This is a common error in chipping because the golfer wants to help the ball into the air and the lower hand gets involved and scoops the ball (1). The moment this happens the loft of the club is influenced and because there is now more loft than there was at address the ball comes up short of the target.

CURE: To prevent this, make sure the grip pressure of the last three fingers of the upper hand is fairly firm. This helps maintain a firm wrist (2). When the chip shot is over, check the back of your upper hand to make sure that it is still flat. If you have trouble keeping the back of your upper hand flat, take an ice-cream stick and tape it to the back of your hand. By practicing with this aid you'll soon get the correct feel. Another helpful aid is to take an elastic band and wrap it around the top of the club and your wrist. If your wrist breaks down while you are chipping, you'll feel the tension in the elastic band change. Work on your chipping until you can maintain a firm wrist.

FAULT: Weight on the back foot.

Many golfers don't realize that their weight is on the back foot until it is pointed out (3). They have subconsciously moved their weight to the back foot in an effort to help the ball into the air.

CURE: Make sure 85 to 90 percent of your weight is on the front foot at address (4), and keep it there throughout the entire shot. If you have a tendency to fall back during the shot, stand with your back foot on its toe. This will ensure that the weight stays on your front foot throughout the shot.

FAULT: Looking up.

This is another fairly common error, and should be the easiest to correct.

CURE: Stay in your posture throughout the entire stroke. When you have completed your follow-through you should still be in the same posture as when you started out. Practice this in front of a mirror to make sure that you are not moving, or get someone to hold your head while you're chipping. This gives you the correct feeling of staying still.

FAULT: Lack of follow-through.

This is caused by lack of trust in your chipping motion and anxiety that the ball is going too far—a shortened follow-through is the result.

CURE: The chipping motion is like a pendulum. A pendulum moves back and forth at the same speed with the same length of backswing and follow-through. The same motion is needed for chipping. If you practice chipping in front of a mirror you can check that your backswing and follow-through are the same length.

FAULT: Lack of pace.

Again caused by lack of trust, the golfer rushes the downswing, hits the ball too hard, or decelerates and hits the ball too soft.

CURE: While making your practice swing back and forth, be aware of the pace of the clubhead (1 & 2). Look at your landing spot while doing your practice strokes and your subconscious will tell you exactly how hard to hit the ball. Be aware of the pace of the club moving back and through and when you are ready to chip, make sure you hit the shot with exactly the same pace as your practice swing. This will give you tremendous distance control with chip shots.

ERRORS IN PUTTING

FAULT: Poor alignment.

This is absolutely the number one fault in putting. Golf is a "sideways-on" game and our eyes are not designed to aim from this angle. When we try to aim the putterface at the hole, we get an optical illusion as to where we are aiming, and most of the time this is incorrect. Golf is the only sport we play "sideways-on". Imagine trying to fire a rifle sideways; it would not be very accurate.

CURE: To rectify this problem put a stripe on the ball. You can buy small plastic devices from golf shops that fit onto the ball and allow you to draw a straight line. When you bend down to place your ball on the green, aim the line on the ball at your intended target. When your putter is behind the ball, make sure the line on your putter is square to the line on the ball.

BELOW: **Align the putter square to the line on the ball.**

FAULT: Breakdown of the wrist.

As with chipping, this is an effort to help the ball towards the hole.

CURE: Apply the same corrections to the breakdown of the wrist in putting as for chipping (see p 205).

FAULT: Eyes following the ball.

When our eyes follow the ball our head moves forward, causing the shoulders to open, the putter head to be pulled offline, and the clubface closes.

CURE: Look at the spot where the ball was after you have hit it. Practice listening for the sound of the ball going into the cup before you look up.

FAULT: Lack of follow-through.

This is caused by a lack of trust and fear of hitting the ball too hard.

CURE: Practice hitting putts where your backswing is half the length of your follow-through. Once you have gained confidence in your distance control by doing this drill you will not quit on your putts.

FAULT: Lack of pace.

The same pendulum motion that applied to chipping also applies to putting. The follow-through should be twice as long as the backswing, but the pace should be even back and through.

CURE: To improve your pace you could buy yourself a metronome. Set it to a steady beat between 60 and 70, for example. End your backswing on one beat and your follow-through on another.

ERRORS IN SAND PLAY

The errors in sand play are similar to the errors found in pitching.

FAULT: Weight on the back foot.
At the address position the golfer tends to leave the weight on the back foot subconsciously thinking that this will help them get the ball out of the bunker (1).

CURE: Make sure the weight is set almost entirely on the front foot with very little weight on the back foot. Keep your weight on this front foot throughout the entire shot (2).

1.

2.

FAULT: Scooping.

This fault relates to having the weight on the back foot (1). The lower hand tries to flip under the upper hand causing the golfer to hit too far behind the ball. The club bounces off the sand and the golfer ends up sculling the ball (3).

4.

3.

5.

6.

CURE: The right hand should cross over the left as it would in a normal pitch shot (4 & 5). The left arm must be extended and both hands finish in front of your body with your weight on your front foot (6).

FAULT: Left arm collapses (7).
Another subconscious attempt to help the ball up into the air instead of trusting the club to do the work.

CURE: Make sure that the left arm stays straight throughout this entire shot (8). Finish with all of your weight on your front foot and with both arms extended out in front of you. Spend some time in the practice bunker until you can do this consistently, and success will be yours on the golf course with this shot.

7.

8.

CALCULATING YOUR SHORT GAME HANDICAP

This is a fun method of improving your short game that helps you recognize how strong or weak your short game really is. You want to keep score of how many shots you take from inside of 50 yards on any given hole. Obviously, on some holes you will hit the green from further out and there would be no short game handicap on that hole.

Below is an example of a scorecard for the first nine holes at Pawleys Plantation Golf and Country Club, showing how to calculate your short game handicap. In the first column on line one is the name of the player, in this case "Mel," next to this is the score and the number of putts on each green. On line two "Drive/GIR" indicates where the drives went and which greens were hit in regulation figures. Line three has "C P B" which stands for chips, pitches, and bunker shots. On the same line the distance finished from the hole after playing the shot to the green is recorded. Line four gives the short game handicap.

On hole No. 1 the player's drive missed the fairway on the left, and hit a 4 iron short of the green.

He played a pitch shot to 10ft from the hole and sank the putt. The score is four with one putt and because two shots were taken from inside of 50 yards, the short game handicap on this hole is two.

On hole No. 2 he hit his drive on the fairway (indicated by an x) and hit a 6 iron to the right of the green. He chipped up to within 4ft of the hole, and sank the putt. So the score was four with one putt, and because of the chip and one putt, the short game handicap on this hole is two. On hole No. 3 he hit a five iron on the green about 30ft from the hole. He then two putted for his par 3. As he had no short game shots from inside of 50 yards, there is no short game handicap on this hole.

On hole No. 4 he hit his drive on the fairway and hit a 2 iron into the front bunker guarding the green. He hit his bunker shot to within 3ft from the hole and one putted for a birdie 4. Again the short game handicap is two. On hole No. 5 his drive was on the fairway, he hit a 7 iron on the green and two putted from 25ft for a regulation par with no short game handicap on this hole. On hole No. 6 he missed the fairway on the left with his drive and hit a 9 iron into the greenside

Hole			1	2	3	4	5	6	7	8	9	OUT
Golden Bear	75.3/146		511	461	194	543	390	432	172	452	416	3571
Blue Heron	72.5/137		495	441	170	498	371	391	151	419	387	3323
White Egret	70.8/130		484	408	162	468	353	382	131	387	358	3133
MEL			4₁	4₁	3₂	4₁	4₂	5₂	3₂	4₂	4₁	35 14
DRIVE / GIR			L45	X6R	5X	X25	X7X	L75	7X	X6X	3w80	5 6
C P B / DISTANCE			P10	C4	30	B3	25	B10	15	30	C6	
Par			5	4	3	5	4	4	3	4	4	36
Men's Handicap			15	1	11	13	5	7	17	3	9	
SHORT GAME HDK			2	2		2		3			2	"5 2.2
Yellow Finch	S: 68.0/123 L: 73.2/131		426	354	127	450	322	367	124	361	351	2882
Red Tail Hawk	70.5/124		395	314	125	419	272	366	124	286	310	2611
Ladies' Handicap			11	1	15	7	5	9	17	3	13	

Date: 1/21/2002   Scorer: Attest:

ABOVE: Take wind into consideration before playing your shot. It may take the ball into some tricky situations.

bunker. He hit his bunker shot to 10ft of the hole and two putted for a bogey 5. He took three shots to get into the hole from inside of 50 yards so his short game handicap on this hole is three.

At the end of nine holes there were five holes in which he played shots from inside of 50 yards totaling 11 shots. Dividing the number of shots, 11, by the number of holes where he played shots from inside of 50 yards, 5, gives the short game handicap of 2.2.

If your handicap is between zero and nine your goal is to have a short game handicap of 2.5 average. If your handicap is between 10 and 18 your goal is to have a short game handicap of 2.75 average. And if your handicap is above 18 your goal is to have a short game handicap of 3.0 average. Start keeping your short game handicap every time you play as this gives you incentive to work on your short game and become a wizard around the greens.

BAD WEATHER GOLF

"When it's breezy swing easy" is another true cliché. Playing in the wind can be daunting for most golfers, but as long as you play your normal game and don't try to overpower the ball the wind is just another test of your ability.

PLAYING IN WIND

In wind, play the ball further back in your stance and take at least one more club, maybe two, depending on the strength of the wind. Then just forget about the wind and make a good golf swing.

When playing downwind be aware that the ball will not stop as quickly so you want to land your ball short of the target to allow for some roll. The wind is also going to carry the ball further in the air so you want to use one less club, maybe two, depending on the strength of the wind.

It is sometimes better to use a 3 wood off the tee instead of the driver when hitting downwind, as a 3 wood will get the ball up into air and carry almost as far as the driver. When playing in a cross wind, take one additional club and aim to a target to the left or right of the fairway or green depending on the direction of the wind. Try to hit the ball directly to this target and do not make compensations in your swing to steer the ball back online.

PLAYING IN RAIN

I don't know anybody who enjoys playing in the rain, but sometimes we are caught in the middle of the round, or, if we are playing in a tournament, we have no option.

Good rain gear is an essential element of playing well in wet conditions. A good rain suit that buttons or zips all way up to the neck and has pockets for balls and tees, plus a large, sturdy umbrella with a towel hung inside on one of the supporting stays will help keep both body and hands dry. It is a good idea to keep a pair of all-weather gloves in your bag for these occasions as well. Nothing is more disconcerting than feeling that the club is going to slip out of your hands during the swing. Carry all of this equipment in your bag if there is even the slightest chance of rain during your round.

Finally, like playing in the wind, keep the swing nice and easy. If you are playing in a tournament, remember that everyone is playing under the same conditions. Accept that your score is going to be slightly higher than normal and stay patient with yourself throughout the round.

BELOW: Warm clothes that keep out the rain are essential on the golf course to ensure an enjoyable game.

COURSE MANAGEMENT

ourse management refers to decision-making by a golfer on club selection and the type of shots chosen when facing the various situations presented during a round of play. A person with good course management skills has the ability to make the right decision for any given situation. Weigh the risk and the reward of each individual shot and evaluate not only your skill level, but also how you are playing on a particular day. If you are not striking the ball well, take less risk; but if you are having a good ball-striking round, sometimes taking a calculated risk will be to your advantage.

On any given day you may be playing your "A" game, "B" game, or "C" game. "A" is when you are playing above average, "B" is playing your average game, and "C" is when you are playing below average. On your "A" days you can take a little more risk and play to a particular side of the fairway or play to tight pin positions. On your "B" days play to the middle of the fairways and greens, and on your "C" days play more conservatively, sometimes even laying up short of the green if there is anything there that could penalize a wayward shot.

The first hole at Pawleys Plantation (see picture left), for example, is a slight dogleg to the right par 5. The best place to be is on the left side of the fairway. Even the rough on the left is a better place to be than the trees on the right. You will be completely blocked out if you go right, but you can advance the ball fairly well up the fairway from the left side rough, or trees. Once you have hit your drive on this par 5, you must decide how to play your

RIGHT: When you feel you are playing well, take a few more risks.

LEFT: The first hole at Pawleys Plantation.

second shot. Can you reach the green in two? If not, put away that fairway wood, take a middle iron and play safely up the fairway.

If you feel you can reach the green in two, be aware that the trouble on this hole has now shifted to the left, where there is out of bounds fairly close to the green. Now it is better to err to the right than the left, so favor the right hand side of the green for this shot. Missing the green to the right will still allow you the chance of getting the ball up and down.

If you have laid up with your second shot, you should now use a pitching or sand wedge for your third. Do not be complacent here. Focus as well as you would with longer shots. Be aware of the wind especially, as a high shot is going to be affected more than your last two shots. Take careful notice of the distance to the flag, not just looking at the distance marker, but to see whether the flag is on the front or back of the green. (This could affect the shot by one or two clubs.) Then, factor in the wind, and select your club. Focus on this shot as you would your drive.

Consider the contours of the green as you are approaching it, as you will see contours from a distance that you will not notice once you are on the green. Look at these undulations both down the line and across the line for a better "feel" for the break and speed. Follow these steps and you'll play your first hole much better. Focus for the rest of the round and your scores will definitely improve.

RIGHT: Heavy rough and bunkers are some of the hazards to be taken into consideration when you plan your shots.

BELOW: Players are wary of the water hazard on this course.

MENTAL ATTITUDE

We all know that golf is a mental game as well as physical, and those who are strong mentally can perform at a higher level. Golfers such as Ben Hogan, Jack Nicklaus, and now Tiger Woods all have an amazing capacity for performing extremely well in pressured situations. Although these players were born with extraordinary skill both mentally and physically, the average player can train himself to be mentally tougher. By understanding how the conscious and subconscious minds interact with one another, the average golfer can learn to not get too mechanical on the golf course and to trust their swing when they need to rely on it most.

THE PROCESS

The golf swing is basically just a motor skill and, in order to learn a motor skill, we first have to do it consciously. Then, as we repeat that motion over and over it will transfer itself into the subconscious where it is stored as a habit, or in the case of the golf swing, a series of habits. So the grip is a habit, the stance is a habit, the takeaway and so on. In order to understand the learning process it is important to understand how habits are formed and how habits manifest themselves. This is particularly important in understanding why we sometimes hit the ball perfectly on the practice range, and then head off to the golf course and play poorly.

Habits are formed when something has happened to us in the past. This happening is recorded in the subconscious and when that situation presents itself to us again we will react to it based on our previous experience. For example, when you walk into a room and see someone you like you will almost immediately smile; on the other hand seeing someone you don't like makes you feel immediately uncomfortable. Our subconscious recognizes certain people based on the information stored there. The subconscious then sends a signal via the nerves to the muscles, and based on our past experience with that person, our body reacts.

As another example, let's refer to the golf course you play on a regular basis. There are certain holes you often play well and there are certain holes that "jump up

RIGHT: A good "mental rehearsal" before you play a tough shot is very important.

and bite you" almost every time you play them. As you walk on to the tee and look down the fairway, the subconscious mind remembers that fairway, that bunker, that tree or that pond. Based on your previous experience on that hole, your body reacts. If you tend to hit a good drive on that hole, you will confidently pull out the driver, step on the tee, and make a good swing. Chances are the drive will go right down the middle. If you tend to play this hole badly, your visual image is poor and you might take a tentative swing with a poor drive as the result.

People often say, "Why does my golf swing feel so much better when I make a practice swing than when the ball is there?" With a practice swing you recognize a non-threatening situation and so the muscles are relaxed and your swing is relaxed. When you take that pace forward and get into your address position over the ball, your subconscious now is receiving a different message. Based on our past experience with that particular shot, the impulse from the subconscious to the muscles will produce a swing that is either good or bad. If we want to improve our shot making on the golf course we first have to improve that picture in the subconscious, and the easiest way to do that is on the practice tee. By improving the mechanics of the swing you'll become a better ball striker and by improving the use of the subconscious mind you'll be a more consistent and tougher player mentally.

The practice tee is where we work on the mechanics of the swing so we are therefore in our conscious mind most of the time. However, once we go to the golf course we need to leave mechanics on the practice tee and switch over to our subconscious mind. We want to think of where we want the ball to go, not how to swing the club. The way to do this is to use what is called a "clear key."

THE 32-BALL DRILL

The 32-ball drill is designed to help you change the established habits you already have to the new habits you are trying to ingrain. This drill was designed by prominent sports psychologist Dr. Cary Mumford.

Lay the balls out into eight groups of four. With the first four balls we are going to be in the mechanical mode—in other words, working on mechanics. You're going to be consciously thinking about what you are doing.

Have two practice swings without the ball, consciously thinking about the swing changes you want to make, and try to feel the new positions. After the two practice swings go ahead and hit the ball, consciously thinking about your new motion. Pull up the next ball, and go through the same thing again, two practice swings and hit the ball. Go through all four balls in exactly the same manner.

The next four balls are going to be hit in the "clear key" mode. A clear key is a key to clear your mind to prevent you from thinking mechanics while you're swinging. We use clear keys every day of our lives; we just don't call them clear keys.

For example, when you're driving along in your car you are not thinking about driving your car. Your mind is on work, golf, and things to do. In other words, you are not thinking of how to drive a car, your motions are automatic. That is a typical clear key. Your mind is preoccupied.

That is what you want to do with the golf swing. Instead of thinking mechanics such as "shift my weight" and "keep my arm straight", you want to block the conscious mind from thinking these things and allow yourself to swing subconsciously.

A clear key is a word or phrase that is used while you're hitting the ball. The definition of a clear key would be "occupying your conscious mind while your subconscious mind performs established habits."

1.

2.

3.

4.

Your clear key could be "Geronimo." From the address position, start your swing saying "Geronimo," to stop your mind thinking of what you are trying to do with the golf swing. You are on automatic. Say the word "Geronimo" three times. The first Geronimo will take you halfway up your backswing (1), the second will take you to the top of your backswing (2). Impact happens on the "ron" of the third Geronimo (3).

If you are saying your clear key at the same pace, and the impact point happens at the same point in the clear key each time, then the pace of your golf swing never changes. You have exactly the same pace in your golf swing from the first tee to the 18th green. Of course, the other benefit is that you are not thinking of the mechanics during your swing and your sub-conscious mind is in control producing a repeating golf swing.

Hit the next ball going through the same thing again. Notice during the clear key mode that there are no practice swings; you're just thinking clear key and nothing else. You can use any clear key you like; however there are two essentials for the clear key.

One, the clear key must be non-golf related; you don't want any words related to the golf swing. And two, try to match the rhythm of your clear key to the rhythm of your swing. If the rhythm of your clear key matches the rhythm of your swing, the pace of your swing never varies from swing to swing. Once you have finished hitting those four balls, go back to the mechanical mode for the next four with the two practice swings in between each shot, the next four back to the clear key mode and so on through the entire 32-ball drill. The goal is to eventually learn to play your entire round in the clear key mode.

Experts say that it takes 21 consecutive days to change a habit, so, if you do not have the option of practicing for three weeks, it is going to take longer. One more thing, while you're in the mechanical mode,

ABOVE: Don't try and analyze why a shot has gone wrong, just take up your practice swing and hit the next one.

stay focused on what you should be doing right and don't get caught up in what you're doing wrong. Don't try and analyze the shot when it goes left, right, fat or thin. Just pull up the next ball, take your practice swings and hit the next one. Remember it took you several years to develop what you have now, so be patient in trying to make these new changes permanent.

PLAYING GOLF WITHIN YOUR PERSONALITY STYLE

If you play golf competitively it is also important to understand how to play within your personality style. Top players in the game today have recognized this factor and all try to "play within themselves" which means within their personality style.

Although there are many personality styles, for the sake of this book we will break them down into four categories.

1. **DRIVER.** These players are "the slashers" and are definitely bottom-line oriented. They play aggressively and tend to be risk takers, sometimes to the point of their own demise. Players that would fall into this category are Arnold Palmer, John Daly, Phil Mickelson, and Lanny Wadkins. All of these players have that swashbuckling style that endears them to the average golfer.

2. **PERSUADER.** These players are "the talkers." Persuaders are fun-loving people who enjoy their golf and treat it as a social occasion even in heated competition. They are usually fairly talkative on the course, and play their best golf when they are in a relaxed frame of mind. Players that would fall into this category are Lee Trevino, Peter Jacobsen, and Fuzzy Zeller.

3. **ANALYZER.** Analyzers are very methodical. They have to have at lot of information at their disposal before they can go ahead and make a decision. Golfers such as Jack Nicklaus, Nick Faldo, Bernhard Langer and Chip Beck would fit into this category.

These are usually the slow players on the golf course and the aforementioned players have been warned about slow play from time to time.

4. **CRAFTSMAN.** These players are "the swingers." They have those syrupy golf swings that look like they are hardly hitting the ball at all. Craftsmen are the easy-going laid-back personalities, very often looking like they don't really care whether they do well not on the golf course. However, don't let this fool you, as these players are just as competitive as everybody else. Golfers who fit into this category include Freddie Couples, Ernie Els and Retief Goosen.

Take this test below to find out what your personality style is.

Circle two words on each line that best describe your personality going across horizontally until you have finished all 15 lines. Add up the number words you have circled in columns A B C, and D and fit them on to this grid indicated below.

A	B	C	D
All Business	Bold	Personable	Deliberate
Organized	Revealing	Courteous	Listening
Industrious	Independent	Congenial	Co-operative
No nonsense	Decided	Talkative	Reflective
Serious	Determined	Warm	Careful
To the point	Risk Taker	Amiable	Moderate
Practical	Aggressive	Empathetic	Passive
Composed	Dogmatic	Emotional	Thorough
Focused	Assertive	Friendly	Patient
Methodical	Assured	Sincere	Cautious
Stoic	Definite	Sociable	Precise
Diligent	Firm	Outgoing	Particular
Systematic	Insistent	Fun-loving	Reasonable
Formal	Confident	Expressive	Hesitative
Persevering	Forceful	Trusting	Restrained

B

```
                                          15|
                                          14|
                                          13|
                                          12|
                                          11|
                                          10|
                                          09|
    DRIVER                                08|                    PERSUADER
                                          07|
                                          06|
                                          05|
                                          04|
                                          03|
                                          02|
                                          01|
A   15,4,13,12,11,10,09,08,07,06,05,04,03,02,01,0,01,02,03,04,05,06,07,08,09,10,11,12,13,14,15   C
                                          01|
                                          02|
                                          03|
                                          04|
                                          05|
                                          06|
                                          07|
    ANALYZER                              08                     CRAFTSMAN
                                          09|
                                          10|
                                          11|
                                          12|
                                          13|
                                          14|
                                          15|
```

D

Put your score from column A on line A, your score from column B on line B, your score from column C on the line C, and your score from column D on line D. Then join the marks to form a square. The biggest quadrant is your dominant style and the next biggest quadrant is your backup style.

Once you have identified your own personality style from this list use one of the players mentioned as a role model, not necessarily for the way that they swing the club, but for how they approach the game. Playing within your style will definitely help you become a better player.

JUNIORS', SENIORS', AND WOMEN'S GOLF

Although children, seniors, and women may differ physically from young men, the basic structure of their golf game remains the same. The key is to develop a good technique.

JUNIORS' GOLF

Junior golfers are much more receptive to change and new ideas. They are also willing to stand and do the same drill over and over (unlike some adults who seek instant gratification).

The development of one particular young girl's swing over the last two years has indicated that if she plays and practices with equal enthusiasm over the next ten years she could compete at a high level. Alexandra Rippy is now 12 years old. When she was nine she was started off with short putts of about 2ft, in order to initiate a feeling of success from the on-set. When a junior sees rapid results their interest and enthusiasm continues, so encourage your child or grandchild with praise for some easy putts. I slowly introduced longer putts, and then moved on to chipping. Using a 7 iron (a proper junior set, not cut offs) we started a few feet away from the putting surface, and kept the chipping motion simple. She was taught to swing her arms like a pendulum and again saw fairly good results in a short time.

After a few weeks with continued work on chipping and putting, she moved on to pitching. The movements became a little more complicated with a wrist hinge and a small body rotation going back and a bigger one going through. In the setup position (1 & 2) her hands are set slightly ahead of the ball.

1.

2.

3.

4.

In the backswing position her left arm is straight, her wrists hinged and her hips rotated back slightly (3 & 4). In the impact position her left arm is still straight, her hips starting to rotate through and her weight shifting onto the front foot (5 & 6).

Just after impact (7 & 8) her arms are extended out in front of her, all the weight through onto the front foot and the hips facing the target.

This was a strong foundation for the full swing to come. By working on this pitch shot (and

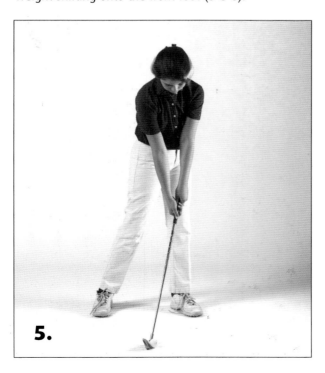

5.

6.

7.

8.

continuing with the chipping and the putting) for about two months, Alexandra was ready for the full swing. It was truly amazing how easily she adapted to the full swing because of the solid foundation she had built with tuition.

All she had to do was make a slightly bigger shoulder turn (9 & 10) to take her to the top of the backswing, and from there she accelerated through the ball with a good body turn.

9.

10.

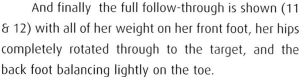

And finally the full follow-through is shown (11 & 12) with all of her weight on her front foot, her hips completely rotated through to the target, and the back foot balancing lightly on the toe.

Build your child or grandchild's swing from the ground up (or in this case from the hole out) and you will be excited with the results. Do not allow them to proceed to the next phase until they have fairly good success with the earlier routines. Enjoy the experience of introducing a young person to this game of a lifetime.

HOW EARLY SHOULD JUNIORS START?

The question often asked by parents and grandparents is how old a child should be before they start golf. Quite honestly, there is no exact age but rather the level of interest. As we all know Tiger Woods started when he was three years old and had tremendous passion for the game that still holds to this day. Fourteen and 15-year-old kids do not belong in golf school if they really do not want to be there, especially if the only reason they are there is that their parents want them to play golf whether they show interest or not.

First of all make sure that the child really wants to play and it is not just a case of the parent taking the child to the course so that the parent can get some golf in. The child must have the desire to play and look forward to the event.

Try not to over-instruct on the course; leave that to the professional. Good course etiquette, fundamental rules and speed of play are important aspects to focus on at an early age. Consideration for other people on the course, and correct pace of play allows everyone to enjoy their golf.

Good behavior is a must. Temper tantrums or sulking should never be tolerated. It is better to remove the child completely from the course and sit down with them at home to explain that that kind of behavior is not acceptable. Make them understand that if this happens in the future they will again be taken home. This might sound harsh, but a sulky child is a pain to play with and a child who enjoys golf without complaining about bad shots is a pleasure to be around. It is important for young golfers to have as much fun as possible. If they are beginners, don't make score an issue. Sometimes pick up the ball and move on to the green and let them putt out to complete the hole. (This will also help speed up play.)

If the child is a reasonably accomplished golfer, then choose stroke play most of the time. Occasionally throw in a few match play rounds, so they get used to competing against an individual as well as the field.

The rules are slightly different in stroke play and match play, so make sure the child knows the differences between them. A video on the rules of golf would be much easier for children to watch and understand than trying to explain the rules to them on the golf course.

Get your child involved in some junior clinics where they can meet other children of similar age and ability. It is much more fun on the golf course for a child who has a friend along that they can compete with or against. Create some friendly rivalry so that not only do they get used to winning graciously but losing graciously as well.

SENIORS' GOLF

As one gets older, there is a tendency to lose flexibility and muscle strength. Unless you work out with weights and do flexibility exercises your golf game is going to suffer as you get older. Practicing alone will not do the job. If you do not work out, at least do some flexibility exercises to increase your range of motion.

Along with a regular stretching routine (see pages 44–49) there are a few other things you can introduce into your golf game that will help you make a better turn on the backswing and develop more speed on the follow-through.

The solution is fairly simple. Simply point your back foot out at about 45 degrees at address, as a friend Calvin Hughes is doing here (1), and turn your front foot out a little more than normal. This foot position will allow you to make a slightly bigger turn on the backswing. Make sure at the top of the backswing (2) that the left arm is fairly straight and there's a

1.

good shoulder turn with minimum hip turn. This will create "torque" or tightness in your torso. The toed out front foot will allow your hips to clear a little quicker on the downswing helping you create a little more clubhead speed. Finish with your body turned completely through to the target with your spine in a vertical position (3). This will reduce the strain on the lower back. Add this to your new-found flexibility, and the long lost distance should return.

2.

3.

1.

WOMEN'S GOLF

Although women have a different physical makeup than men, the basic structure of the golf swing is exactly the same. For most women, because of a lack of physical strength, their main problem is distance. Distance can be created by good technique, and here are the most important aspects for creating good clubhead speed.

In the address position make sure that the left arm is fully extended creating a straight line from the left shoulder all the way down to the ball (1). Weight should be even front foot to back foot with the knees only slightly bent. Too much knee bend will restrict a good shoulder turn on the backswing.

The start of the backswing should be as wide as possible creating a wide arc by keeping the left arm straight and allowing the right arm to fold very slightly (2). It is important at this point in the backswing to restrict the hip turn in order to create some tension in

2.

3.

4.

the torso when you reach the top of the backswing (3). It is also important to maintain the position of the right knee by keeping the weight on the inside of the right foot. This prevents the hips from swaying laterally and allowing the weight to go to the outside of the right foot which creates problems when you try to start the downswing.

At the top of the backswing the left arm is still fully extended with a full shoulder turn (3). There is plenty of distance between the arms and the body. At this point the muscles in the torso should feel tight,

wound up like a rubber band ready to unleash all the energy created by the good backswing.

At impact, the weight has shifted to the front foot (4). The hands still lead the clubhead, creating a slightly downward blow and ensuring that the loft of the club is being fully utilized. Note that there is no breakdown of the left wrist which would add loft to the club, which in turn would mean a loss in distance.

Through impact the arms are still fully extended, again creating as wide an arc as possible. It is critical in this area that the left arm does not break down.

5.

6.

Note that the right hand is crossed over the left indicating a full release ensuring that the clubface is square at impact. The head is still down, with the eyes looking at the spot where the ball was and allowing the right shoulder to come under the chin. This position ensures that a good spine angle is maintained throughout the hitting area (5).

Finally, the follow-through (6) finishes with all the weight now on the front foot, the hips completely turned through to the target and hands finishing slightly above the head. This follow-through position

indicates a good rotation of the torso through the hitting area which is vital if clubhead speed is to be created. At this point, the golfer can pick up her back foot and not lose her balance. Do this little test next time you are on the practice tee to see whether the weight shift is correct or not.

If you cannot lift your back foot at the end of your follow-through you have not shifted the weight correctly, not turned your torso quickly enough, and therefore you have not hit the ball with your maximum potential.

NUTRITION

What you eat either on the golf course or prior to playing golf directly impacts your capacity to concentrate, your ability to control your golf swing, the ability to control your temper, and your level of energy throughout the round. The majority of professional golfers are all very conscious of their diets, as it will increase their potential to win.

Water has a great impact on performance on the golf course. Particularly when playing on a hot day, the body will dehydrate through perspiration and exhalation. If this fluid is not replaced sufficiently, the body cannot perform at its optimum level and a decrease in performance will result.

The ideal drink on the golf course is bottled water with added electrolytes, also called mineral water. As spring water does not necessarily contain minerals, choose brands that are labeled "mineral" water. Our bodies depend on electrolytes to transmit nerve impulses and maintain muscle function. If these electrolytes are not replaced as we are playing, the impulses from the brain to the muscle are affected and precise movements such as the putting stroke will be the first to suffer.

Potassium is a mineral connected with muscle coordination. We lose potassium through perspiration, so we need to take steps to replace this important electrolyte with potassium rich foods that can be easily consumed on the golf course, such as sunflower seeds, bananas, and carrots. The ideal scenario when playing on very hot days would be to drink several bottles of mineral water during the round while snacking on these foods.

LEFT: Eating pasta before a game will maintain your energy levels.

RIGHT: A nutritious diet will enable you to enjoy your golf game to the max.

Elite athletes have strict diet programs to help enhance performance. To most people golf looks like a fairly sedate sport, but it too demands focus, concentration, and perfect muscle coordination. For those of you who would like to perform at a higher level, eat before and during play.

Including flax seed and lecithin in your diet supports the operation of nerve fibers in the brain. Lecithin is important in the relaying of messages through the nervous system, improving muscle coordination. Performance enhancing herbs are found in power bars and sports drinks. Gingko biloba increases mental alertness, kava kava, and ginger work together as a relaxant, maca promotes clear thinking, and camu-camu controls anxiety. Rhodiola rosea herbal extract influences learning and memory by supporting neuro-transmitters and influencing brain chemistry.

FOODS TO HELP WITH STIFFNESS

Stretching daily is highly recommended, and will increase flexibility and reduce muscle tightness. Muscle tightness on the golf course not only hampers a smooth, fluid golf swing but can leave us prone to injury. Since many of us race from our car to the first tee we should eat foods that help, not hamper the situation. Avoid foods that contain high levels of uric acid such as red meats, dairy products, and caffeine. By drinking plenty of mineral water on the course and avoiding dehydration, you can also prevent injury.

As you get older, diet should play a bigger part not only in your golf game, but in your lifestyle. Cut back on red meats and increase vegetables, nuts, fruits, and wholewheat breads. Add supplements such as amino acids, alfalfa, and wheat grass. Some

ABOVE: Bananas are rich in potassium, a mineral that is lost through perspiration.

LEFT: Raisins are good to eat while you are on the golf course to enhance performance.

of the pros on the Senior Tour are great advocates of this. Bob Charles, now in his mid-60s and still playing great golf, takes supplements such as velvet antler and shark cartilage.

For those of you who suffer from fatigue late in the round, avoid foods that are high in sugar and resist drinks such as beer, tea or coffee. Increase potassium intake, found in bananas, energy bars, raisins, and mineral supplements. Mineral water is a far better alternative to highly sugared drinks.

FOODS TO ENHANCE PERFORMANCE PRIOR TO PLAYING

Oatmeal, eggs, whole wheat toast, honey, peanut butter, turkey, smoked salmon, and fish are excellent foods to eat before play. Drink mineral water or unsweetened fruit juice.

Whether it is breakfast or lunch you are having, make sure you finish your meal at least one hour before your tee time.

FOODS TO EAT ON THE GOLF COURSE

Apples, pears, peanuts, granola bars and muffins (without sugar added), slow-release energy bars, raisins, bananas, and carrots are good snacks on the golf course.

FOODS TO AVOID ON THE GOLF COURSE

Avoid sugared drinks, such as fruit drinks, caffeine, and alcohol and food additives such as aspartame, (an artificial sweetener) MSG (a flavor enhancer), and hydrolyzed vegetable protein (used in soups). These all affect brain function to some degree.

FOODS TO EAT THE NIGHT BEFORE

Eat slow-release energy food such as pasta, meatless lasagna, fish, salads, vegetables, rice, broccoli, cauli-flower, and sweet potatoes.

ABOVE: Dried apricots are a good way of introducing more fruits into your diet as they make a tasty snack.

LEFT: Increase the amount of fruits in your diet, such as grapes, and avoid high sugar foods.

RULES AND ETIQUETTE

In order to have a level playing field in any endeavor there must be rules. Golf is no exception. When it comes to the Rules of Golf most people play in complete ignorance. Not because they are cheaters but because the rules of golf seem so complicated. Although there are only 34 golf rules there are so many sections and subsections that they can be complicated even to an experienced professional golfer.

Of course, trying to read a rule book is about as boring as watching paint dry. However, there is a book published by the U.S.G.A. called "Rules and Decisions." This is a compilation of letters written into the U.S.G.A. asking for rulings on particular situations. At any given time, due to the fact that there are thousands of golf courses throughout the world and hundreds of golfers playing each course, weird occurrences are sure to present themselves. By reading these questions and answers on the rules of golf, you can learn more in an hour than spending days trying to figure out the rule book. At tournaments throughout the world both amateur and professional rules officials are on hand to help with decisions relating to the rules. So, although the rules may be complicated, each golfer owes it to himself and his fellow competitors to know at least the basic ones and also correct etiquette. Playing the game will be more fun for all.

The following are a few basic rules for situations that you will encounter regularly on the golf course.

1. **PLAY THE BALL AS IT LIES.** This is probably the most basic rule in golf but one that is ignored by many recreational golfers. Once you have teed off, keep playing the ball as it lies until you have holed out. This is the only way to play if you want to keep a measure of your true ability (i.e. don't move the ball to any other spot that you deem easier to hit from.)

2. **UNPLAYABLE LIE.** Occasionally on the golf course you are going to find your ball in a situation where you are unable to play it. It is important to understand the three options available to you in this instance.

A) **Stroke and distance.** You may return to where you played your original shot and replay the shot adding one penalty stroke.

B) **Two club lengths not nearer the hole.** You may drop the ball two club lengths from the spot where the ball lay and add one penalty stroke (1 to 4).

C) **Go back as far as you like.** You may take your ball back as far as you like keeping the point where the ball lay between yourself and the flagstick. Again add one penalty stroke.

3. **OUT OF BOUNDS.** On most courses there is an external boundary and if a ball crosses this line you will have to replay your shot from the same spot adding the stroke and distance penalty, which equates to two strokes. On some of the more modern golf courses where housing communities exist, out of bounds markers can be found on almost every hole.

ABOVE: A ball is out of bounds when it is outside the line drawn from the external edge of the out of bounds post.

Homeowners do not want golfers in their manicured gardens and playing shots out of the rhododendrons, so golf course committees deem these areas out of bounds. Again the stroke and distance penalty will apply. To clarify, if you hit a ball out of bounds, play another ball and add two strokes to your score. A ball is out of bounds when the entire ball lies outside the line drawn from the external edge of the out of bounds post. If even a small part of the ball is inside this line, the ball is still considered in bounds.

4.   **WATER HAZARDS:** There are two types of water hazards and different rules apply.

A) Lateral water hazards. A lateral water hazard is one that runs alongside the hole— either a river, stream, lake or pond (1 & 2 overleaf). A lateral water hazard will be marked with red stakes or a red line. When your ball enters a lateral water hazard, you may drop the ball one club length from the edge of the hazard at the point where the ball entered the hazard. If you wish, you may also drop a ball on the opposite bank directly across from that spot. Add one penalty stroke to your score.

B) **Water hazard.** A regular water hazard is a river, stream, lake or pond that lies directly between you and the hole, and will be marked with yellow stakes or a yellow line. When your ball enters a water hazard, you may drop the ball not nearer the hole, keeping the point where the ball entered the hazard between yourself and the hole. You may go back as far as you like. You must add one penalty stroke.

GOLF ETIQUETTE

Golf course etiquette is just plain common sense. But to help out new golfers, who may not understand some of these strange rituals, here are some very important points of etiquette.

1. Always stay behind the person playing his or her shot. Golfers do not have perfect control of their shots so stay behind in order to stay out of harm's way. Many unnecessary accidents on the

golf course over the years could have been avoided by remembering this simple rule.

2. Keep quiet. It is just good manners to be quiet when someone else is preparing to play their shot. Golf is a game of concentration, and it is certainly difficult to concentrate if one of your playing partners is chatting away.

3. Keep play moving. Remember that it is your obligation to maintain reasonable speed of play by keeping up with the group in front of you. If no one is in front of you, do not hold up the people behind you. If you are playing in a foursome, a reasonable pace of play would be about 15 minutes per hole which equates to a four and a half hour round. If you are a beginner, and have difficulty maintaining this pace, pick up your ball when you have played more than two strokes over par.

4. Rake bunkers after you have played your shot (3). Nothing is more annoying than walking into a bunker and finding your ball in someone's divot or foot print.

TYPES OF MATCHES

STROKE PLAY. This is the most common format for determining a tournament winner. You simply count the strokes on each hole from the tee into the cup. Add up the total for 18 holes to get your gross score, and then subtract your handicap to determine your net score.

MATCH PLAY. The match is determined by the number of holes won, and not by the number of strokes. The match is usually between two players, but if the match is best ball, it can be between four. The lowest score on the hole wins the hole and the match is over

when someone is more holes up than there are holes left to play. So if a player is five holes up with only four holes left to play he is declared the winner by five and four.

CAPTAIN'S CHOICE. This is a great format for company outings and tournaments that include many high handicap or beginner golfers. All golfers tee off and the best shot is selected with all players playing their second shot from that spot. Again the best shot is selected and the hole is played in this manner until the ball is in the cup. This is a fun tournament for beginners, as they do not have to keep their individual score, but can contribute to the team with an excellent shot here and there.

FOURSOMES. This is an alternate shot format where player No. 1 tees off, player No. 2 plays the second shot, player No.1 then plays the third shot, and they play alternate shots until the ball is in hole. If player No. 1 tees off on the first hole, then player No. 2 will tee off on the second hole. No.1 will tee off on the odd holes, and No. 2 will tee off on all the even holes.

HANDICAPS

A handicap is determined by taking your gross score, subtracting the stroke rating of the golf course you have played, and the resulting figure recorded. You then take the best ten scores out of the last 20 rounds to determine your handicap.

Handicaps are used in order for all players to compete equally against one another. A person who has not been playing very long and has a high handicap can compete against someone who's been playing for years and has a low handicap. At the end of the day the person who has played best relative to his handicap is the winner.

Imagine a beginner tennis player trying to play against Andre Agassi. No matter how many points Andre gave, the match would be no contest. However, a 36 handicapper competing against Tiger Woods could score 105, and if Tiger scored 70 he will have lost. Golf is one of the few sports in the world where beginners and world champions can compete against one another, because of our handicap system.

For the handicap system to work everyone needs to be honest. There are unfortunately some among us who feel the need to win at all costs. With a little dishonesty they see to it that a false score is recorded thus giving them a higher handicap. We call these people "sandbaggers." They intentionally miss putts when they do not count, and will often go out and play by themselves and not return their scores for handicap purposes. Fortunately, these people are few and far between, and for the most part golfers are an honest bunch. Even top professionals, playing golf for a living where each shot could mean thousands of dollars, call penalty shots upon themselves when there have been no witnesses to the violation. Sometimes people not even involved in a match have called attention to rules infractions. There has been an occasion where penalty shots were applied to a player, who inadvertently and unintentionally broke a rule, because a television viewer had noticed and called in to the Rules Committee.

In the final analysis, each player must be true to themselves, play their best golf at all times and record their scores honestly so that we all can compete against each other on any given day on any given course.

TEN FAVORITE COURSES

The phrase "horses for courses" is very true. You will notice on the PGA Tour that certain players play better in some events than others. This is because certain characteristics of a golf course allow a player with a particular game style to play better on that course. For example, Mark O Meara has played particularly well at Pebble Beach, and Ben Hogan played Riviera so well they called it "Hogan's Alley." Augusta National suited Jack Nicklaus particularly well with his high ball flight and Bruce Lietske plays courses with holes that are shaped primarily from left to right, suiting his natural ball flight. Courses that were shaped from right to left would suit players such as Arnold Palmer and Gary Player who have right to left ball flights. Players such as Lee Trevino and Bobby Locke played well in the British Open because of their lower ball flights. The following are the author's top ten public or semi-private courses and a guide to scoring well on them.

1. BALLYBUNION
Ireland

This is a classic shotmaker's course. To score well here you have to possess the ability to hit every shot you ever learned. High shots are needed downwind in order to hold the fast and sometimes raised greens and low shots are needed to penetrate the wind that is almost constant on the seaside links. Keeping the ball in play is a must as the rough is punishing. You do not need to be very long off the tee on this course, and at 6,593 yards from the back tees and 6,241 yards from the "members" tees you can score fairly well if you keep the ball out of the heather. In the final analysis, to score well you need patience and lady luck on your side.

2. ST. ANDREWS
Scotland

This classic links course is wide open with generous landing areas and fairly flat greens. Again, like Ballybunion, keeping the ball in play is priority number one, but this time the key is location of your drives. There are many punishing fairway bunkers at St. Andrews and although it's longer than most Scottish courses at 6,933 yards, the fairways are usually hard which makes the ball run a long way. Herein lies the trouble at St. Andrews, because a running ball inevitably falls into a deep fairway bunker. Even the great Jack Nicklaus has taken more than one shot to extricate himself. The real secret to playing well at St. Andrews is to hire a good caddy. A caddy guided the author around the course with 2 irons, 3 woods and only the occasional driver off the tee, keeping out of fairway bunkers for the entire round.

Putting at St. Andrews requires a deft touch as the greens are fairly quick, but extremely true, so if your caddy reads the greens well you'll have a good putting day. In conclusion, keep the ball out of the bunkers and invest in a class "A" caddy at St. Andrews.

BELOW: **The golf course in St. Andrews, Scotland has a very old and palace-like clubhouse.**

3. PINEHURST NO2
North Carolina, USA

This is as close as the average golfer will ever get to Augusta National; both courses are very similar from tee to green. With beautiful wide fairways, not overly long at 6,309 yards off the "white" tees or all the way back at 7,189 yards and with generous landing areas, you can use a driver off most tees. The keys to good scores at Pinehurst No2 are good iron play to put the ball on the correct area of the green (again, similar challenges to Augusta) and good course management. If you do miss a green, you do not want to miss it on the wrong side. All the greens on this Donald Ross design are raised and great chipping and even greater putting are required if you are to shoot below your handicap.

ABOVE: The fairway for the 17th hole at the Pinehurst Resort and Country Club designed by Donald Ross.

In the final analysis, good course management and a gentle touch around the greens will reward you with a pleasant experience. A wonderful sense of history and tradition greets you as you arrive at the elegant clubhouse.

under the lip and have to play the ball backwards into the center of the bunker in order to give yourself a chance at your next shot. Royal County Down is also home to a large fairway bunker —it is at least 15ft deep. Just don't go there.

In the final analysis, drive it long and straight, hit good iron shots and chip and putt well. Other than that it is a piece of cake.

4. ROYAL COUNTY DOWN
Newcastle, Northern Ireland

This is definitely one of the toughest golf courses, and at 7,037 yards is an extreme test of good ball striking and of one's patience. Even the ladies' tees measure over 6,000 yards and a beginning golfer must be armed with plenty of balls. Driving the ball straight off the tee is a must on this heather and gorse lined course, and hitting accurate iron shots to well bunkered greens is required. The greenside and fairway bunkers are all "natural" meaning that the grass around them is unkempt. Your ball may roll

5. HARBOUR TOWN GOLF LINKS
Hilton Head Island, South Carolina, USA

Home to the Heritage Classic on the PGA Tour, this is a course that David Love III really owns. He has that long high drive, and this is the secret to playing Harbour Town. The fairways are tree lined and fairly narrow, but at 6,916 yards you have to be able to hit the ball long to score well. Davis' high tee shots give him the length required, but because the ball does not roll very far, it stays out of the semi-rough which consists of pine needles that have fallen off the

ABOVE: Two golfers and a dog walk on the fairway of the ninth hole at the Royal County Down Golf Club.

majestic pine trees. Harbour Towns' greens are small, so a premium is placed on accurate iron play. If you are wild off the tee, take plenty of balls to help you finish the course. The 18th hole is one of the best finishing holes in tournament golf.

6. PAWLEYS PLANTATION
Pawleys Island, South Carolina, USA

Pawleys Plantation is the author's home course. This is a Jack Nicklaus design and because of Jacks preference to fade the ball you'd think that most holes would be shaped left to right, but Pawleys Plantation actually suits a golfer who draws the ball.

This is another tough golf course where a pre-mium is placed on good tee shots. The course is not long from the member's tees at 6,127 yards, and off the back tees is 7,026 yards. Pawleys suits the golfer who drives the ball long and straight, and a good aggressive putter would do well here as the greens are fairly flat and medium paced. John Daly or Retief Goosen would score well here. Would Tiger Woods score well here? Tiger can score well anywhere.

7. THE EUROPEAN CLUB
Brittas Bay, Wicklow, Ireland

Expecting a typical "American" course (confusing it with the "K Club" in Ireland), The European Club was a pleasant surprise. It is a great links course set on the Irish Sea and although a fairly young course, plays more like a course that has been there for centuries. That is a compliment to the designer who used the natural terrain to create this masterpiece. If ever you go across to Ireland, the trip would not be complete without a visit to The European Club.

At 7,149 yards off the back tees this can be a monster if the wind is blowing, which it often does in Ireland. The member's tees are a little more generous at 6,186 yards, but to play this course well you need to keep the ball low. The bunkers are placed to the sides of the greens, and the fairways are closely mown. This allows the golfer to play his approach shots low into the green, landing them short, and letting them run onto the putting surface. Fairly flat greens with a medium pace help an aggressive putter score well here. Paul Azinger with his low boring tee shots and great putting stroke would have great success here.

8. OLD HEAD GOLF LINKS
Kinsale, County Cork, Ireland

The "Pebble Beach" of Ireland, Old Head is a golfers dream come true. At 7,215 yards, this course can be almost unplayable in a howling wind, but by using both blue and white tees on the correct holes, it is playable in any conditions.

The fairways are fairly generous, and the greens large, so you can keep the ball in play without any problem. The biggest challenge is that the views on almost every hole are so spectacular they distract you from your game. Take a camera along on this outing.

Good ball striking from a golfer who does not try to "force" the pace will result in a good round. Ernie Els with his beautiful fluid swing would do well

BELOW: Old Head sits on the coastline giving the golfer spectacular views.

here as would Retief Goosen and Freddie Couples. A golfer with a fast swing will not last the pace and will be many over par by the time they get to the 17th hole. The entire hole is set on the side of cliff. In the final analysis, keep a good rhythm, be patient, and enjoy the view.

9. HUMEWOOD GOLF CLUB
Port Elizabeth, South Africa

Humewood is one of those courses you will always remember because it leaves you feeling like a young man after his first date—breathless and anticipating the next date.

It is not a long course, but like so many, it's a great ball striker's course. You need all the shots in the bag if you want to score well. On a Saturday you could hit a drive almost to the first green, leaving yourself a short chip, and on Sunday morning hit a drive and a three iron and still not get there. The legendary Bobby Locke once said that he felt this was such a true test of golf that the British Open should be played here every year. A shorter hitter such as Brad Faxon or Loren Roberts would do well here, because they will not hit a lot of greens in regulation and putting is at a premium.

10. DURBAN COUNTRY CLUB
Durban, South Africa

This course is ranked as the number one course in South Africa, with several South African Open Championships being played here over the years, and rightfully so. A great test of golf, you have to drive the ball straight here. Both sides of the fairway are lined with heavy bushes, which is extremely punishing. Once you have driven the ball on the fairway, you'll find the greens are smaller than normal, so the need for accurate iron play will test your patience. A great iron player such as Hale Irwin would have done well here in his prime and the legendary golfer Gary Player won several S.A. Open Championships here.

CONTACT INFORMATION

If you would like more information contact:

Mel Sole
The Phil Ritson-Mel Sole Golf Schools
P.O. Box 2580
Pawleys Island, SC 29585

Toll Free: 1-800-624-4653
Local: 843-237-4993
Fax: 843-237-8397

Email: info@ritson-sole.com
Website: www.ritson-sole.com

PHOTO CREDITS

The publisher wishes to thank Simon Clay for taking all the photography in this book. Other photographs were kindly supplied as follows:

Front cover photograph: © Duomo/CORBIS; page 9 courtesy of Chrysalis Images; pages 10 and 11 courtesy of Hulton|Archive; pages 81 (top right, bottom left and bottom right) courtesy of Bill Woodward; page 240 courtesy of Digital Vision; page 250 courtesy of Michael S. Lewis/CORBIS; pages 251 and 252 courtesy of © Tony Roberts/CORBIS; page 253 courtesy of © Michael Brennan/CORBIS.

INDEX

accessories 30–31, 36–39
accuracy 190–192
address position 70–71, 79, 235
address position, errors in 186–189
alignment 65, 66–67, 72, 122, 208
analysis 43
arc, increasing width of, drill 89
arm plane 79
Augusta National, 249, 250
Azinger, Paul 253

backswing 76–78
bad weather 214–215
balls 12, 22
ball above feet 162
ball below feet 161
Ballybunion 249
baseball drill 89
baseball grip 63
basic rules 242–246
bicep curl 52
Blackheath Common 10
Blackheath Golf Club 10
body line 65, 76
British Open 10, 249
"brush brush" shot 114
bunker shot, greenside 132–137
bunker, ball in back of 146–147
bunker, ball near face of 143
bunker, buried lie in 144
bunker, long pitch from 144–145
bunkers, fairway 138–140

casting 80
"chicken wing"
   (see wrists, breakdown of)
chipping:
   6-8-10 method 112
   bellied wedge 116
   errors in 205
   fairway woods 116
   important aspects of 115
   practicing at home 120–121
   table 112
   technique 114
   Texas wedge 117–119
classes, size of 42
clear key 222–224
clothes 24

clubs 12–19
collapsing left arm 191,199–200, 212
Company of Edinburgh Golfers 10
contours, green 218
Couples, Freddie 76, 97, 254
Curtis Cup 11

Daly, John 252
divot repair tool 31
downhill lies 160
downswing 80–81
draw, hitting an intentional 149–150
drills 89–91
drive 71
Durban Country Club 254

elastic band, using a 115, 205
Elbow Tic-Tac 32
electrolytes 238
Els, Ernie 76, 97
e-mail 43
equipment 12
equipment, choosing 23
etiquette 246–247
European Club, The 252–253

facilities 43
fade, hitting an intentional 151–152
Faxon, Brad 254
fiberglass 19
flagstick, playing close to 141–143
flexibility 44–49, 234
follow-through 82, 86
follow-through, lack of 207, 208
foods:
   for stiffness 240–241
   to avoid 241
   to eat on the golf course 241
   to enhance performance 241

Gentleman Golfers of Leith 10
gloves 22, 27
golf bags 28–29
golf balls 12, 15, 22
golf clubs 15
Golf Magazine 43
golf school, choosing a 40
golf swing 61–62
Goosen, Retief 252, 254

"gouf" 8
graphite 19
grip thickness 23
grips 20, 63
gutta ball 12
gutta percha 12

habit, 220, 224
handicap, calculating your short game
   213–214
handicaps 248
Harbour Town Golf Links 251–252
hardpan, hitting off 148
Haskell 12
heavy rough, playing out of 154–155
hickory 12, 13, 19
high shots 164–165
   ball position 164
   club selection 164
   weight distribution 164
history of the game 8–11
Hogan, Ben 220, 249
Home Gym 50
hooking 175–177
Hoylake 10, 12
Humewood Golf Club 254
hybrid clubs 16

impact position 80
inside-out clubhead path 81
interlocking grip, the 63
irons 12, 14–16

juniors, how early to start 232
juniors' golf 228–233

K Club 252
King James II 8
King James VI (James I) 10
King William IV 10
"kolven" 8

Ladies Golf Union, The 10
left-handed shots 153
length 23
lessons 40
lie angle 23
Lietske, Bruce 249
lob shot 108–109

Locke, Bobby 249, 254
Love, David III 251
low shots 166–167
 ball position 166
 club selection 166
 follow-through 166
 key factors 166

Mary Queen of Scots 8
matches, types of 247–248
 captain's choice 247
 foursomes 248
 match play 247
 stroke play 247
Meara, Mark O 249
"middleclubs" 111
Muirfield 10
Mumford, Cary 222
Musselburgh 10

Nicklaus, Jack 76, 220, 249
North Devon Ladies Club 10

Old Course 8
Old Head Golf Links 253–254
Open Championship 12
open stance 69
"over the top" 80, 191
overlapping grip, the 63
overswinging 181–182

pace, lack of 207, 208
Palmer, Arnold 249
Pawleys Plantation 216, 252
persimmon 12
personality style 225–227
 analyzer 225
 craftsman 226
 driver 225
 persuader 225
PGA Tour 249
philosophy, school's 40, 42
Pinehurst No.2 250–251
pitch shots, scale of 111
pitching:
 7-8-9 distance method 104–105
 errors in 199–204
 key features of 106–107
 technique 102
Player, Gary 254
position:
 ball position 71, 131
 ball position (fairway woods) 92
 bottom hand 64–65
 club 76

hand 70, 188
 top hand 64–65
posture 70, 87–88
 putting 130
potassium 238
power, gaining 190–192
practicing 56–58
 at home 59–60
pre-shot routine, 72–73
Prestwick 10
pull hook 177
pulling 173–174
push hook 175–176
pushing 178
putters 21
putting:
 alignment 122
 developing "feel" 128–129
 drills 124–129
 errors in 208
 push drill 124–125
 repetitive putt drill 126–127

rain, playing in 215
reverse pivot 78, 183–185
Roberts, Loren 254
Royal and Ancient Golf Club of St.
 Andrews 10, 11, 15
Royal Calcutta 11
Royal County Down 251
Royal Montreal 11
Rules of Golf 10
Ryder Cup 11

sand play, errors in 210–212
scooping 204, 211
seniors' golf 234
shaft: 19
 angle 80
 flex 23
 plane 79
shanking 197–198
Shepard, Alan 11
shoes 22, 26
slicing 168–172
Society of St. Andrews' Golfers, The (see
 Royal and Ancient Golf Club of St.
 Andrews)
Solheim Cup 11
spine angle 201
St. Andrews 8, 10, 11, 249–250
St. Andrews Club 11
stance 68–69, 70, 186–187
 square 69
 closed 69

steep slopes 163
strength exercises 50–53
stretching 44–49, 234
subconscious 220, 222
swing plane 79, 96
swing weight 23
swing, 90 percent 97
swing, fairway woods 94–95
swing, full 97–101

takeaway 74
target line 65, 76
technique 61
technology 42
Texas wedge 117–119
Tin Cup 32
topping 179–180
torque 78
Toski's Touch 34–35
Trevino, Lee 249
trollies, electronic 30

U.S. Open 96
United States Golf Association 11, 15
uphill lies 159

videotapes 39, 40, 43
visualization 72

Walker Cup, The 11
warming up 54–5
water hazards 245–246
water, mineral 238
water, playing out of 156–158
wedge, lob 110
wedge, pitching 110
wedge, sand 110
wedges 18, 110–111
weight shift 78, 82–84, 86, 193–196,
 206, 210
"whoosh" drill 89
wind, playing in 214
women's golf 235–237
woods 15, 16
woods versus irons 96
woods, fairway 71
Woods, Tiger 220, 232, 252
World War I 15
wrist cock 76
Wrist Tic-Tac 34, 36
wrists, breakdown of 115, 199–200, 205,
 208

yardage meter 31